## Counseling in Secondary Schools:
## A Frame of Reference

# Counseling
# in
# Secondary Schools

## A Frame of Reference

**JOHN W. LOUGHARY, PH.D.**

*Supervisor of Guidance and Research*
*San Bernardino City Schools*

HARPER & BROTHERS, PUBLISHERS, NEW YORK

COUNSELING IN SECONDARY SCHOOLS: A FRAME OF REFERENCE

Library of Congress catalog card number: 61–5452

*To my wife, Josephine,*
*and our children, Kate, Kevin, Patrick, Rebecca, and Kelly*

# CONTENTS

# PREFACE

As I have assumed the successive roles of school counselor in preparation, practicing school counselor, teacher of school counselors, and supervisor of school counselors, I have been constantly impressed with one idea. A great number of trained, prepared, accredited school counselors lack adequate concepts of what they hope to accomplish by counseling with students. In their noncounseling guidance responsibilities, the lack does not seem evident. The objectives here are often well thought out and stated in meaningful terms with which school counselors can feel comfortable.

What many school counselors lack and need is a counseling frame of reference, one that is appropriate to the kinds of problems which they encounter, and consistent with the type of institution in which they work. The primary objective of secondary schools is to educate young people, not to cure them. It is true that educators have reached the general conclusion that many young people cannot achieve educational objectives without assistance in solving personal problems. Many counselors have therefore been assigned the responsibility of helping these young people. Nevertheless, the primary counseling contributions of most school counselors are expected to be developmental rather than remedial or preventive. At the same time, the contribution of the school counselor must be different from that of the classroom teacher. From this is derived the contention that the school counselor, in order to offer effective counseling assistance, needs a counseling frame of reference from which he can provide primarily developmental counseling help to young people in secondary schools.

The objective of this book is to provide one such frame of reference and to discuss and illustrate its applications. I certainly do not mean to suggest that the frame of reference presented is the only one available or appropriate for school counselors. It is my hope that whether the frame of reference itself is accepted or rejected, the process by which the reader-counselor arrives at a decision will involve some constructive thought. The purpose of the book will be served if the reader develops a counseling frame of reference which he can accept and effectively employ in his own counseling with secondary school students.

Two assumptions are basic to the counseling frame of reference developed in the following pages. One is that the most important function and the greatest potential contribution of a school counselor is counseling per se. The other is that while noncounseling guidance procedures make valuable contributions of their own, they should all facilitate counseling efforts. Thus, readers who subscribe to what seems to be a current trend towards viewing school counselors primarily as guidance consultants who spend the majority of their time helping teachers will undoubtedly find this frame of reference difficult to accept. The position taken here is that while counselors do many things, all of which are not counseling, they do, in fact, spend more time counseling with students than in other guidance activities.

There are several reasons for contending that counseling per se should be the main function of school counselors. First, the counseling session is perhaps the only situation in the school in which students can be accepted without evaluative regard for their aspirations, achievements, or overt social behavior. This is not to say that teachers are not warm and friendly towards students, but only to suggest that teaching and cocurricular activities must necessarily involve a communication of teachers' evaluations of students. This is certainly desirable for many reasons, but each student should also have some opportunity in school to be accepted as he is, without personal evaluation. Second, counselors have competencies not generally possessed by other faculty members for helping students learn to make effective personal decisions. The counseling session is the situation in which these competencies are most effectively employed.

School people often note that "every teacher is a counselor" and that much counseling is done by teachers outside of the counseling office. Certainly it must be acknowledged that teachers and administrators provide valuable noninstructional assistance to students. They offer advice, support, friendship, and reinforcement to students, and such assistance may be called counseling. The premise of this book, however, is that a distinction should be made between the friendship offered to students by teachers and administrators, and the systematic attempts of a counselor, employing certain competencies, to help students solve problems within a counseling interview. It is the latter kind of help which I choose to call counseling.

It may be well to state several tasks which have not been attempted in this book. There is no systematic attempt to review the general principles and concepts which are basic to almost all nonanalytic theories of counseling, except as this is necessary to clarify the frame of reference discussed. These concepts are more than adequately covered by writers such as C. H. Patterson, Francis P. Robinson, Carl Rogers, and Leona Tyler, to name only a few. Nor is there any attempt to discuss principles of school guidance, except in Chapter 7, where relationships between noncounseling guidance procedures and the frame of reference are treated. The literature abounds in books on principles. Similarly, concepts and methods of noncounseling guidance procedures as such, for example, appraisals and placement, are not discussed. Again, many excellent books devoted to these functions are available. Finally, there is no attempt to review counseling research literature, or to present a bibliography of such literature. The authors mentioned above, and others, have done this admirably. The few suggested references at the ends of most chapters are included because they can be particularly valuable to school counselors. Each of these references includes extensive bibliographies of theoretical, procedural, and research literature.

Like most authors of textbooks, I am greatly indebted to many people. An attempt to list them all would only result in omitting many. I have leaned heavily on the writings of Wendell Johnson and E. Lakin Phillips. My associations as a student, friend, and colleague of Kenneth B. Hoyt at the State University of Iowa contributed immensely to my ideas on counseling in secondary schools. As is true of most counselors, my greatest source of enlightenment has been those with whom I have counseled. The assistance of Mrs. Anne Wolf during the initial stages of writing is gratefully acknowledged.

JOHN W. LOUGHARY

*San Bernardino*
*January, 1960*

# Counseling in Secondary Schools:
## A Frame of Reference

....................................................................

# CHAPTER 1

# Counseling Responsibilities of Secondary School Counselors

---

## SOME CONTEXTS FOR COUNSELING

The occupation of secondary school counselor varies to a startling degree in job content and emphasis from one counselor to another and from one school system to another. Consequently, the student preparing for a career as a school counselor can have only a vague notion of what he will actually be doing once he obtains a school counseling job. For example, a counselor may be assigned counselees of one or both sexes. He may be concerned with various kinds of problems, or he may be restricted to dealing with students who state only a single type of problem, such as college selection, course selection, or personal adjustment. Besides these differences in counseling responsibilities, there are differences among school systems in the amount of counseling time assigned. Thus the counselor's assignment may vary from less than an hour a day to full time. If he is not a full-time counselor he may have a variety of other duties, such as teaching one or more subjects, administrative duties, attendance work, or even driving a school bus.

A further consideration is the way the counselor is expected to spend whatever time he is assigned for counseling. In some schools all of his time is to be spent in counseling sessions. In other schools he may have such guidance responsibilities as directing a testing program, scoring tests, preparing student transcripts, or helping teachers with guidance units. In one school system or another, all of these functions are part of the counselor's job.

These guidance responsibilities of the secondary school counselor, varied as they are, can generally be classified as either counseling re-

1

sponsibilities per se or noncounseling guidance duties. This book is concerned primarily with the first type of responsibility. Noncounseling guidance activities have been discussed in many excellent guidance textbooks. The reader is invited to use the annotated bibliographies following several chapters of this book as initial guides to developing an understanding of these noncounseling aspects of guidance.

The purpose of this chapter is to help the reader understand the various kinds of counseling aids that the secondary school counselor should provide to students. The headings of the subsections are not intended to be a classification of adolescent adjustment problems. Such clinical categorizations are available and can make a real contribution to the counselor's understanding of students.[1] The discussion that follows consists instead of illustrations of circumstances or contexts in which students may be expected to manifest problems. The underlying contention is that to understand his function, the school counselor must appreciate the importance of these situations, which are particularly applicable to secondary school students.

## Aptitude and Achievement

Ted was 20 years old and had been attending high school for 3 years. His cumulative folder included two Otis IQ's, both under 90. The majority of his marks were D's, with F's in math and English, a C in shop and B's in physical education. He failed Grades 1 and 5.

Ted was popular with his fellow students and had been an outstanding athlete. His age prevented him from participating in school athletics during his senior year.

During his first three years in high school several teachers had referred Ted to counselors because of his failing work. Counselors found Ted pleasant, but not particularly interested in discussing his future school work or plans.

During the middle of the first grading period of his senior year, Ted became very discouraged about his failing work in several classes and suggested to one teacher that he might not finish school. The teacher advised him to see the counselor. By this time Ted was very

[1] Francis P. Robinson, *Principles and Procedures in Student Counseling,* Harper, 1950, chap. 3. Professor Robinson's brief discussion of the bases for categorizing counseling problems is valuable reading for the beginning school counselor.

much concerned about his future and went to the counselor seeking help.

Betty was in the first year of high school. She had entered from a local junior high, where her marks had been very low. On reviewing her cumulative folder, the high school counselor found three obtained IQ's, all over 145. The folder also contained letters from Betty's parents written over the years, showing concern over her low achievement and asking for advice. Teachers' comments in the folder indicated that several had tried to encourage greater achievement from Betty but had failed. Betty's standardized achievement test scores in most areas were far above her grade-level placement.

Bob was a junior at City High. He had been absent from school for several weeks and his parents had asked the counselor for an appointment. They stated that Bob was so discouraged over his progressively declining grades that he would not go to school.

The counselor reviewed Bob's cumulative folder and found several IQ's obtained over a ten-year period. All of these were around 105. Bob's grades presented an interesting pattern. During elementary school he was a straight A student. His junior high grades were mostly A's with a few B's. During his first year in high school he received one A, three D's, and two C's. During his sophomore year he received one B, four C's, and one D. Teachers' comments throughout the years praised Bob's conscientious school work. Upon entering high school Bob completed a questionnaire in which he indicated his three occupational choices as engineer, physician, and chemist. He had been taking a college preparatory program.

These three students had at least one thing in common. Each came to the attention of the counselor because of an aptitude problem, an achievement problem, or both. As the counselor worked with each of these students, it became more obvious that the aptitude-achievement problem was only one aspect of each case. Ted, for example, had failed for years to do some honest thinking about his school performance and his vocational future; Betty, it developed, had a home life full of conflicts and tensions; and Bob had failed to adjust his aspirations in view of the evidence regarding his abilities.

Nevertheless, the high school counselor first becomes involved with many counselees from the perspective of an aptitude-achievement problem. While additional aspects of such problems are often identified and are the concerns of the school counselor, because of the context in which he works he ultimately must help such students solve their aptitude-achievement problems.

## Peer Relations

Barbara was referred to the counselor by her eighth-grade social studies teacher. Barbara was an excellent student and showed talent in many nonschool activities, such as piano and voice lessons. However, she was constantly involved in arguments with her classmates. She attempted to take part in school extracurricular activities, but immediately met with hostile feelings from her peers. Teachers reported that they had difficulty getting other students to work with Barbara on class projects. When the situation got to the point where other students were becoming aggressively hostile towards Barbara, she was referred to the counselor.

Jim was an above-average student with real leadership ability. He was quite sophisticated for his age and demonstrated mature judgment in influencing his peers. Consequently, teachers had encouraged his leadership activities. Jim had been successful in obtaining statewide positions in student government organizations.

At the beginning of his senior year Jim was a candidate for student body president. He had only token opposition and the school staff looked forward to working with Jim as the elected leader of his peers. To their great surprise, the students elected Jim's opponent by a large majority. Jim's immediate discouragement was expected. However, he began to spend less time with his peers and within two months had withdrawn from all student activities and spent no more time than regular school hours with his former associates. Jim's friends and teachers became concerned and informed the counselor of the situation.

Carol was a pleasant and capable girl. She was enrolled in the commerical program in high school and looked forward to working for several years after graduation before marrying. The senior office practice teacher was impressed by Carol's ability and hoped to place her in a good job upon graduation. In a short time, however, she became increasingly concerned about Carol's self-confidence. She noted that Carol vacillated between a healthy, realistic degree of confidence in herself and moods of self-degradation. The teacher could not understand the inconsistency in view of Carol's high achievement, and she consequently consulted the school counselor.

During the initial counseling interview Carol related embarrassment over her father's laboring job, her parents' limited education, and the generally low cultural standards of their home. What she could not understand, and what had become an increasing worry to her, was that some days she felt completely inferior to her fellow students and believed that none of them thought very much of her, while on other days she had none of these feelings.

The problems suggested in these brief case descriptions, like those in the previous context, are complex and involve many aspects other than those mentioned. However, they serve to illustrate another context in which the school counselor begins to work with students. One of the main functions of school is to help students learn to relate themselves to other people. Although school is certainly more than a "preparation for life" (it *is* life), students by definition are immature and are developing the skills and knowledge necessary to adult living. The process is complex and frequently confusing. As a result, the school counselor has numerous opportunities to help students who, for various reasons, find aspects of their development particularly difficult.

## Vocational Objectives

Henry was a student of high ability and achievement. His parents were both well educated and his father was a teacher. During the ninth grade Henry planned with the counselor his four-year high school program. He wanted a traditional college preparatory program, which the counselor thought was appropriate. During subsequent contacts with Henry the counselor brought up the subject of vocational interest. Henry had a number of vocational interests, including law, dentistry, and physics. He believed his high school work would allow him to enter college programs in any of these fields and was anxious to take a liberal arts course for a year or two before deciding upon a career. Henry's parents indicated to the counselor that they approved of their son's plans.

At the beginning of his senior year Henry applied to several universities for admission. He also applied to various sources for financial aid. He was offered admission to a prominent out-of-state university and to a liberal arts college in his state. He was offered adequate financial aid if he would enroll in the large university as a physics major. While the liberal arts college offered him financial aid without obligation as to a major field of study, the amount of aid would have to be supplemented from other sources. Both schools wanted an immediate decision from Henry, and he came to the counselor for help.

Harold was a boy of moderate ability with no interest in college. He had varied work experiences and decided that he wanted something other than outside work as a life's vocation. His parents insisted that Harold's high school education be practical and lead to something other than a blind-alley job. Harold agreed with them and asked the high school counselor what courses he should take in order to reach his vocational goal.

Jane was a senior in high school. She had average intelligence and achieved at an expected level. She was physically unattractive and lacked personality characteristics that might have compensated for her physical appearance. She had few interests and was practically unnoticed by her peers.

In a scheduled interview with the school counselor for the purpose of post-high-school planning, Jane stated that her vocational interest was marriage and homemaking. She indicated a realistic appraisal of her current status, and felt that she had to make some changes if she were ever to realize her ambitions. She asked the counselor for help in formulating a vocational plan.

Selecting an occupation, needless to say, is a very involved process. It begins soon after birth, with the development of attitudes, and for many people it goes on through later adulthood. The time an individual spends in high school is a crucial period in the process for several reasons. With the trend toward occupational specialization, skills learned in high school become more important. The situation is complicated by demands for post-high-school training of one sort or another. An increasing number of high school students must pursue a program preparing them for additional training which will, in turn, allow them to enter an occupation of their choice. Obviously the situation for many is not clear-cut. Much post-high-school training is on-the-job training, and an individual stands a greater chance of being admitted to various on-the-job training programs if he has had certain kinds of secondary school preparation. In other words, he looks better or worse to various employers depending upon his high school program. From this perspective it should be evident that helping a student plan his high school program is not a simple, routine task. Because of the many and vital vocational implications, it is an important counseling task demanding the best skills and knowledge of the counselor.

Nonclassroom activities also contribute to the individual's vocational development. During the high school years the student is given greater freedom and opportunity to experiment with interests and personal relations. The extent and kind of experiences he has will influence his further vocational development.

The three cases described above illustrate these points. The necessity for Henry to select a college faces him with a major choice point in his career. If he chooses the prominent university he commits himself to vocational objectives laregly determined by the immediate goal of easing the financial burden of a college education. How important is this goal in the long run? What are the other criteria that should be considered? To view Henry's case as a routine advising problem is an indication of poor insight. The counselor assumes a serious responsibility when he agrees to help Henry.

Harold illustrates a kind of vocational choice problem frequently encountered by high school counselors. Counseling with Harold led to considerations other than those stated before Harold was able to come to grips with the stated vocational problem. Harold's stage of vocational thinking is typical of a great many high school students. Too often these youngsters receive only superficial counseling (usually advice). Interpreting some test data and suggesting pertinent occupational literature is inadequate. The Harolds in the country do not want to attend college and only infrequently make a major contribution to society. But as a group they represent the majority of us. If they are to be a stable and strong majority, it is important that as they make plans for entering the vocational arena, they understand themselves and the complex world of work.

More often than not, the sort of problem illustrated by Jane never comes into the clear focus of counselors or other school personnel. The Janes are around and many of them finish high school almost unnoticed.

They are not dated and in general are excluded from the very kinds of school activities which could make significant contributions towards their vocational development. Great strides have been made towards making adequate curricular provisions in recognition of the idea that housewife is in every sense of the word an occupation. This is good. Nevertheless, an equally important part of the occupation of housewife involves the personal relations so important to family stability and happiness. Many things which contribute to healthy personal relations can be taught. On the other hand, personal relations are also attitudes based on experience, and although many high school girls and boys have opportunities to gain such experience, many do not. More important, those who do not are often the very people who most need such experience. The counselor, then, can help by making opportunities for important experiences available, and can supplement these by helping the Janes to understand and accept the circumstances which limit their opportunities.

## Other Contexts

The three general areas illustrated above represent three contexts within which high school counselors most frequently have initial contacts with a student. Case descriptions from less frequent contexts are given below. The first illustrates the student with a disability; the second, the student having difficulty orienting himself to a new school; and the third, the student whose problem is not actually related to a school situation but who comes to the counselor for help.

Tim was a senior in high school. When he was 9 years old an accident resulted in amputation of his right arm. He was the youngest of seven siblings, and had lived with his tenant-farmer parents until he finished the eighth grade, and then moved to town and lived with an older brother. The brother provided little supervision, but did keep Tim in school. When the brother married, Tim's sister, Mrs. Brown, and her husband agreed that Tim could live with them while he completed his last year of high school. Tim moved several hundred miles to live with the Browns.

Tim was pleasant and easy to get along with. He was appreciative of the help Mr. Brown was giving him, and assumed responsibility for chores around the home. Tim had little interest, however, in planning for the future. He stated during his first session with the counselor that he really did not know what he wanted to do. He blamed no one for his disability and did not give any indication of feeling sorry for himself. Although he seemed to accept his disability, there was evidence to suggest that he had not thought about its implications. It was not that he had repressed his problems, but rather that he had never been strongly motivated to think about vocational plans, and thus had not seen his disability from a vocational perspective.

Norma transferred from a small high school in a southern state to a medium-size midwestern high school at the beginning of her senior year. She was a straight A student and had been taking all college preparatory courses. Her father and older sister were both in medicine and Norma had aspirations to become a physician.

The midwestern school had a college preparatory orientation and about 80 percent of its graduates enrolled in college. Norma was particularly pleased with the prospect of attending the new school. During the first week of the semester her counselor scheduled an orientation interview with Norma. He found her very quiet, but alert and optimistic. At mid-semester the counselor reviewed the marks of all new students in school and discovered that Norma was receiving C's in most of her courses.

A second interview was scheduled with Norma. The counselor found a very worried and confused girl. Norma stated that the amount of work and standards of achievement were much more demanding than in her former school. She was working late every evening and during week ends to complete her assignments. She was particularly discouraged over the relative ease with which other students met scholastic requirements. In attempting to analyze her difficulties she indicated that during the past three years she had done little writing, her science and mathematics courses had been almost entirely a matter of memorization, and she had no background in social studies. Thus, in addition to not being able to keep up, she was having doubts about her own adequacy. Partly because of the pressure of course assignments, she had made no social contacts with her classmates.

In reviewing her cumulative folder the counselor found that Norma had scores on a standardized achievement test comparable to scores of the better students in the new school. He also found information from her former school indicating that while she was quiet, she had been popular and had played significant roles in student activities.

Tom was a junior in high school and had talked with his counselor several times about education plans. Shortly after school started in the fall, Tom saw the counselor in the hallway and asked for an appointment. When he arrived for the appointment he was vague about his purpose. Eventually he related a story about seeing his father with another woman on several occasions during the past summer. Tom had discovered that his father had been seeing a lot of the woman, and that she had accompanied him on out-of-town business trips. He was also sure that his mother knew nothing of the situation.

Tom was confused and wanted help. He was angry and hurt by his father's actions and was embarrassed and worried for his mother. He had considered talking with both his mother and father about the situation, but could not convince himself that such action would be wise, even if he could carry it through. He was taking the counselor into his confidence and wanted help.

Admittedly, problems in such contexts as these are encountered less frequently by the high school counselor. Nevertheless, by the very nature of the relationship which he establishes with students, he can expect them to come for help with problems such as these. Failure to respond in a helpful way is inexcusable in terms of both the counselor's responsibility and the respect he must have from students if he is to accomplish his purposes.

A final context should be mentioned, although it is not parallel to those already discussed. As a counselor gains the respect of a group of students he will probably receive an increasing number of general self-referrals. The term *general* is important. Although a number of students come to counselors voluntarily to discuss a particular problem, many come only for a general talk. Just as the physician has patients who come in "just to be safe," the school counselor has students who come in just to talk things over. Some of these students have serious conflicts and decisions facing them, but many do not. In the former group the counselor will meet students who are searching for values, experiencing conflict over religious beliefs and affiliations, questioning the standards of their peer group, or facing a similarly important choice.

Among the latter group of students are those who simply want and need to relate to an accepting adult. They have no serious problem, but perhaps as a result of a counseling experience they gain in greater clarity of thought and insight about themselves. There are also a few students in this group who can develop into "professional counselees." Their stated problems are superficial and they show little interest in actually solving their problems. However, their persistent attempt to gain the counselor's attention is in itself an indication of need for help of some kind.

## A MORE STRUCTURED VIEW

Thus far in this chapter we have attempted to describe the counseling responsibilities of the secondary school counselor in terms of selected case examples. The discussion should benefit from a somewhat more structured examination of the several contexts within which the school counselor meets the problems of students. What follows is not meant to be a prescription for organizing counseling responsibilities. It is simply an attempt to outline their general scope.

The secondary school counselor differs from counselors in other situations in that he himself takes responsibility for initiating a large proportion of his interviews. The exact proportion depends on his point of view, his particular school population, and the kind of relationship that he has been able to establish with students and teachers in general. It is the rare counselor, however, who can fulfill the program outlined below without initiating many interviews himself.

Most counselors will meet the majority of their students for the first time in brief orientation interviews. Probably little actual counseling takes place in these interviews, but they are nevertheless important as preparation for the counseling contacts that the counselor will have with students during their secondary school careers. The interviews are brief, usually no longer than 15 minutes, and generally serve to (1) let the student know that someone is available for counseling and interested in him as an individual, (2) indicate the purposes of counseling to the student, (3) uncover immediate orientation problems, and (4) provide the counselor with a few minutes in which to become acquainted with the student and vice versa.

The first actual counseling interview that a student experiences is probably for the purpose of planning a long-term program of studies. Educational counseling, as it is commonly labeled, should involve more than the selection of courses. In these interviews the counselor may find it necessary to help the student achieve better self-understanding and self-acceptance before adequate course planning can be accomplished. Consequently, during educational counseling sessions, personal, family, and vocational problems are frequently discovered.

Insofar as scheduled interviews are concerned, the third context in which the counselor will see students is in post-high-school planning interviews. Typically, these are held with each student at the beginning of his senior year. This practice indicates a poorly organized counseling program. There is a great deal more sense in beginning post-high-school planning during educational planning interviews. That is, if each year the counselor provides each counselee with an opportunity to review his educational plans, a natural consideration of the review should be postgraduation plans. When this procedure is employed, students can do continuous evaluative planning in terms of vocational as well as educational objectives.

In addition to working in these contexts, the counselor as a matter of course will hold scheduled interviews with failing and underachieving students, and with students identified through the appraisal program as needing help of various kinds. The counselor who has developed good relationships with other professional school personnel will have students representing a variety of problems referred to him by teachers, medical personnel, administrators, and attendance personnel. In addition, up to the limits of his "public relations," the counselor will receive referrals from parents and from nonschool professional personnel, such as judges, social workers, and police. Finally, the counselor will see students within the context of general self-referrals.

## SUMMARY

In this chapter we have provided a brief look at the scope of contexts within which the secondary school counselor encounters students with problems; we have also impressed upon the reader that counseling with secondary school students should be more than advising. Although the majority of problems encountered by counselors working with adolescents may be rightfully described as typical (in the statistical sense), their typicality does not lessen their importance. They have serious and far-reaching implications. Students will achieve some degree of solution to their problems without the help of counseling. The purpose of secondary school counseling is to help adolescents learn to solve those problems better.

••••••••••••••••••••••••••••••••••••••••••••••••••••••••••••••••••••

# CHAPTER 2

# A Frame of Reference for Secondary School Counselors

The purposes of this chapter are threefold. The first is to point up the importance and unique status of decision making for adolescents. The second is to develop the idea that most problems of adolescents can be reduced to decision-making problems. The final purpose is to present a counseling frame of reference for viewing the decision-making problems of adolescents.

## MAKING DECISIONS DURING ADOLESCENCE

The observation that it is typical for adolescents (and people of all ages, as a matter of fact) to have psychological problems has been made previously. Another way of stating this is that at various times everyone experiences some degree of psychological discomfort as a result of behavior which does not confirm various self-estimates. Life is just not so simple. In order to avoid psychological discomfort, one would always have to be in a position to make perfectly adequate decisions about each situation in which he found himself. This, of course, is seldom if ever the case. An individual is never in a situation identical with a past situation. Circumstances may be, and quite often are, similar to previous sets of circumstances; but each new situation is approached with some degree of ignorance. Consequently, each new decision is based to some extent on inadequate information (experience), or uncertainty.

There are at least three indications that the uncertainty element of decision making is especially important during adolescence. In the first place, the adolescent is suddenly faced with the responsibility for making many of his own decisions. He is asked, for example, to indicate a vocational interest, and is expected to assume responsibility for selecting his school courses. He must decide how to divide his limited time among many activities; he must make decisions regarding immediate versus future rewards, and many other matters. The mere fact that he is expected to make important decisions and be responsible for entailed behavior represents a major change in the life of the beginning adolescent.

In the second place, although he has been making minor decisions for some time, these have been limited for the most part to the relatively narrow range of his immediate needs. As the individual enters adolescence, the range in which he is expected to make decisions is greatly enlarged. The consequences of decisions are not as easy to see as they previously were. He finds that many of the needs about which he must make decisions are not complementary, but often in direct though subtle conflict with one another. Thus, not only are there more decisions to make, but they are decisions of a much more complex nature than he has previously encountered.

Third, the adolescent, faced with this increase in the number and complexity of his decisions, lacks decision-making experience. Making appropriate decisions is not an easy task. The ability to make decisions wisely is based on experience, and on skill in getting maximum feedback from experience and adjusting subsequent decisions accordingly.

Decision-making during adolescence has broad significance. The decision may have significance for the adolescent's immediate behavior. For example, the high school freshman deciding to pursue a college preparatory program when he lacks the necessary scholastic aptitude to do will suffer some immediate consequences. Among these might be worry and unhappiness over his probable low achievement, feelings which could in turn prevent him from taking advantage of immediate learning opportunities appropriate to his abilities.

Often closely related are the decisions made during adolescence which have real significance for adult life. The high school girl, for example, who is bright and likes school, but who decides to get married rather than finish school, makes a decision which has far-reaching effects. A more common illustration is that of the capable high school student who decides in favor of an easy high school program as opposed to more rigorous academic courses. If it is recognized that after high school graduation he may choose to attend college, his decision is seen to have many implications.

Finally, decision-making experience in itself is significant. The extent to which adults can make appropriate decisions is a major determinant of the satisfaction they achieve from living. The adult who fails to develop decision-making competencies during adolescence will be handicapped in dealing with the complexities of adulthood. Those who do develop these decision-making competencies during adolescence will have a firm basis for continued development during their adult years.

## THE DECISION-MAKING CONSTRUCT

The concept to be developed in this section is that the problems of secondary school students which the counselor encounters can in large part be reduced to decision-making problems. The contention that student problems are not so simple, though granted, is irrelevant to this discussion. To say that most problems can be reduced to decision-making problems is only to suggest that there is a level of abstraction at which each problem is similar. At the operational level, each problem is unique. In abstracting we provide a construct which will give some order to the otherwise infinite number of specific problems. Such orderliness at an abstract level should enable the counselor to understand better what kinds of help counselees need. Given this general understanding, the counselor should be in a better position to derive methods for helping individual counselees.

Perhaps the best means of clarifying the decision-making construct is an illustration. Take, for example, the problem of Barbara, as stated in Chapter 1: Barbara was referred to the counselor by her eighth-grade social studies teacher. Barbara was an excellent student, and showed talent in many nonschool activities, such as piano and voice lessons. However, she was constantly involved in arguments with her classmates. She attempted to take part in school extracurricular activities, but immediately met with hostile feelings from her peers. Teachers reported that they had difficulty getting other students to work with Barbara on class projects. When the situation got to the point where other students were becoming aggressively hostile towards Barbara, she was referred to the counselor.

As the counselor worked with Barbara her problems became

better defined and the various aspects could be differentiated. First of all, Barbara felt that she was the brightest student in her grade and expected her classmates to accord her the role of intellectual leader. Her self-estimate was not realistic in terms of several criteria that were available. Although she was a bright girl, several of her classmates were superior in terms of measured scholastic aptitude. The outcome of these circumstances was Barbara's resentment of the lack of the status which her self-estimate justified.

A second aspect of her problem centered around her musical talents. Having had successful experiences outside of school in musical activities, she expected to meet with similar success at school, but her classmates were not willing to grant her automatic status. They expected her to earn whatever status her talents would allow. Barbara failed to appreciate the social aspects of the situation and thus misunderstood and resented the reactions of her fellow students.

A third aspect of Barbara's problem stemmed from differences between the social structure of her home life and her school life. Her father and mother were separated; the older siblings lived with the father, and Barbara lived with her mother. Barbara's mother was a competent and active woman. Her many interests, however, forced responsibilities on Barbara which were atypical for her age. She was left to care for herself much of the time, and often she had only her own wishes to consider. Within relatively broad limits, Barbara was her own master. The majority of her classmates, however, had more definite and restrictive limits set by their parents. In addition, their home lives involved cooperative family planning and consideration for the desires and activities of other family members. Thus the attitudes towards cooperation held by the majority of students were at considerable odds with those held by Barbara, and her dictatorial and autonomous behavior was resented by most of her peers.

Now, can this problem, complicated by several aspects, be reduced to a decision-making problem? First, consider the needs involved in each aspect of the problem:

| *Problem Aspect* | *Needs* |
|---|---|
| A. Inappropriate self-estimate of scholastic ability. | 1. Information about scholastic abilities. |
| | 2. Information about other qualities important to leadership. |

| *Problem Aspect* | *Needs* |
|---|---|
| | 3. Understanding of adolescent subculture mores. |
| | 4. Insight regarding effects of behavior resulting from inappropriate self-estimate. |
| B. Recognition of musical talents. | 1. Understanding of different values given to these talents by various people. |
| | 2. Understanding of the nonmusical aspects of school music activities. |
| | 3. Insight regarding the reactions of students to her attempt to transfer status from one context to another. |
| C. Regard for desires of others versus regard for one's own desires. | 1. Realization of her relative freedom from parental authority. |
| | 2. Appreciation of the effects of nondemocratic behavior in a democratically oriented peer group. |
| | 3. Understanding of the way in which her specific behavior is perceived by her peers. |
| | 4. Understanding of the needs that she is attempting to satisfy by her dictatorial behavior. |

This presentation of Barbara's case is admittedly general and oversimplified. However, enough of the pertinent data are given to allow an illustration of the decision-making construct. The counselor can do several things to help Barbara achieve more appropriate behavior. That is, he can help her achieve the needs that have been listed. For example, various kinds of appraisal data can help correct the self-estimate. Provision and discussion of information on adolescent mores can help Barbara to define the subculture in which she lives. Effective counseling can provide a means of achieving insight on the reactions of peers to her behavior.

Although all of these things are appropriate counseling functions, they are only preliminary to an actual solution of the problem. These functions, taken separately or collectively, do not solve the problem. In the final analysis, the solution can be achieved only through decisions made by Barbara. Her decisions will presumably be more appropriate when made after counseling has helped Barbara satisfy the needs listed; but it is the decisions, not the satisfaction of the prerequisite needs, that represent the *sine qua non* of solving personal problems.

The following list of alternative decisions is limited and represents only some of the decisions that Barbara could make. However, they serve as illustrations.

| *Problem Aspect* | *Possible Decisions* |
|---|---|
| A. Inappropriate self-estimate of scholastic ability. | 1. To work towards being a member of the high achievement group.<br>2. To withdraw from attempts to work with other students.<br>3. To continue present attempts to lead high achievement group.<br>4. To use different method to achieve leadership status in high achievement group. |
| B. Recognition of musical talents. | 1. Not to participate in school music activities.<br>2. To accept the nonmusical aspects of school music activities and participate on that basis.<br>3. To continue participating on the same level.<br>4. To work towards changing the nature of school music activities. |
| C. Regard for desires of others versus regard for one's own desires. | 1. To continue autonomous and dictatorial behavior.<br>2. To self-impose parental limits of peers.<br>3. To restrict autonomy and accept group decisions.<br>4. To withdraw from any attempts to work with peers. |

The decision-making construct helps the counselor and the counselee to estimate the potential decisions that the counselee can make. By attempting to see the various aspects of student problems as counseling progresses, they both can list (mentally at least) various decisions for each aspect. Having begun to do this, they have some realistic bases for giving structure to a particular counseling case. This is not to suggest that the counselor should then become completely directive in his efforts to help the student. This would obviously result in his taking the responsibility for problem solving away from the counselee. On the other hand, the employment of the decision-making construct offers the counselor suggestions as to what kinds of help he should be providing. For example, does the counselee need information in order to make his decision, and if so, what kinds? Does he need help in accepting certain of his characteristics before making a decision? Does he need help in gaining self-confidence before he can make decisions? The student's thinking is aided in a similar manner.

It should be recognized that the counselee does not make these decisions at a given point in time. Most decisions involve a process. A given decision is related to past decisions and will be related to further decisions. As stressed earlier, the decision-making construct is by definition an abstraction. It will not serve to make counseling with secondary school students mechanical. It does not provide the counselor with a means for providing answers to student problems. It is, in a sense, a tool which the counselor can use to give some order to the problems of students.

The exact way in which the tool is used will depend as much on the skills and idiosyncrasies of a particular counselor as it will on the problems and personality of a particular student. For instance, a given counselor working with a given student might, as counseling progresses, talk with the student in terms of the decision-making construct. A different counselor, or the same one, working with another student, might never talk in terms of decision making, even though he employed the construct in thinking about the student's problem. It is up to the individual counselor to decide how he will use the construct, if indeed he finds it helpful and chooses to use it at all.

## A FRAME OF REFERENCE

In the preceding section the contention was made that counseling with high school students can become more definitive when their problems are viewed from the decision-making construct. In this section we shall attempt to provide an operational frame of reference for high school counseling. Like that of the more general construct discussed above, the purpose of an operational frame of reference is not to make counseling mechanical, but simply to provide a means for giving additional order to counseling so that the counselor can achieve greater effectiveness.

In general, high school counselors appear to lack a meaningful frame of reference from which to counsel with students. What perspective they have tends to be based on a vaguely understood conglomeration of Rogerian techniques, depth theory, and advice giving. The absence of a frame of reference can be accounted for in several ways. First, many high school counselors have arrived at their jobs with little, if any, specific counseling preparation. These people typically have spent a number of years as classroom teachers. Quite often, because of their success in teaching, administrators have rewarded them with counselorships. Thus, although many of these persons have a tremendous backlog of experiences with adolescents and their problems, they are frequently naïve about effective ways of helping students solve their problems, they lack the necessary environmental information used in counseling, and, more important, they bring to counseling the job expectations of teaching, which often conflict with those of counseling. Fortunately, school officials have recognized some of the differences between counseling and classroom teaching and are making accordant provisions in state certification requirements (although most of these are far from perfect).

Second, training programs for secondary school counselors typically emphasize the noncounseling aspects of guidance to the neglect of counseling itself. Third, it is usually difficult to establish a realistic supervised practicum situation in a training program, and thus secondary school counselors-in-training fail to obtain adequate supervised practice. Fourth, when the training program does include courses in personality theory and related areas, these are usually limited to survey type courses.

For all these reasons, when the trained counselor begins his career in the secondary school he is least prepared to carry out the counseling responsibilities of his job. Quite naturally, then, he concentrates on those things with which he is most familiar and comfortable, and as time goes on he is even more reluctant to counsel. In essence, the experience from which a frame of reference could develop is never obtained. The result is that when the counselor does encounter students with problems, he feels inadequate. Yet, because of his sincere desire to help, he does whatever he can. He reflects and restates ideas and remains silent without really knowing why. He searches for causes in a confused estimate of the student's repressed experiences and unconscious motives, and finally in desperation and self-defense gives him

advice. There are, of course, many high school counselors whose preparation and counseling do not fit this description, but such persons
certainly do not make up a majority.

The need for a counseling frame of reference is specifically evident when we consider a particular characteristic of secondary school
counseling, namely, that the high school counselor has relatively limited contacts with his counselees. If, for example, a counselor is responsible for four hundred students, he will have only several contacts with
each student during the three or four years of school. If he is to help
students, he must be able to do so in a limited amount of time. High
school counseling, for the most part, is necessarily short-term counseling.

Most counseling theories are not suitable for use in high school
counseling because of the relatively long-term counseling they imply.
Depth therapy can go on for several years, and by definition could
not be limited to only one or two interviews. Rogerian theory and practice, though not requiring as much time, still involves a prohibitive
amount for general use by high school counselors. What is needed is a
frame of reference from which one can counsel effectively, on a short-
term basis, with high school students having typical problems.

Other writers concerned with broader aspects of counseling and
psychotherapy have recently raised questions about the validity of
depth therapy and long term nondepth therapy. They have also suggested that the constructs of depth-oriented psychotherapies are un-
necessarily complex, and propose that it is possible to counsel effectively from a much more economical and scientifically testable set of
constructs. This "new view" of counseling permits and even encourages short-term counseling.

The clearest and most complete statement of this view of counseling, is probably that of E. Lakin Phillips. In his book, *Psychotherapy,
A Modern Theory and Practice,* Dr. Phillips develops what he refers
to as interference theory, and provides numerous illustrations of its
applicability. In Phillips' own words: ·

In the interference theory, behavioral possibilities are seen as being selected by the perceiving-acting person (not by his unconscious mind) to meet
the situations that confront him. Instead of behavior being a function of what
lies in the mind's "depths" it is regarded as a function of what the person sees
as the possible effectiveness of the kinds of behavior within choice range. These
are matters of the organism's perception—an on-going, living, choosing proc-

ess—not a matter of relatively static, deep-rooted layers (processes or entities) in an unconscious mind.[1]

If one is going to change a person's behavior, he has to interfere with what the person is doing, with his assumption-system, with his assertions, or with their degree. The clinician teaches the patient to bet less, or to bet on different probabilities.[2]

In the interference theory we can see our way to conducting psychotherapy on a more practical basis; we do not set up mind-structure so formidable that it has to be beaten down or broken into a defenseless position, or plumbed to its depth. We can change probabilities of behaving by rather modest, practical, and surprisingly economical and efficient means. We can apply psychotherapy to far more people, under less austere and expensive conditions, and we can relate psychotherapy to the host of knowledge we have from other areas of science.[3]

The last quotation from Phillips suggests that his concern is much broader than the relatively limited interest of this book. Thus, the discussion that follows deals with those ideas which seem to have particular applicability for secondary school counseling. The theoretical considerations and side issues of interference theory are excluded, not because they are unimportant. They are important, and many readers will want to refer to Phillips' book. The purpose here, that of providing a frame of reference for school counselors, can be accomplished without an explicit examination of the technical aspects of interference theory.

The basic tenet of interference theory is that because behavior is on-going it can best be understood in terms of an individual's current status. To examine past behavior in order to understand current behavior is held to be unnecessary, and possibly misleading. An individual behaves in certain ways because of his current needs, goals, and beliefs. To help the counselee achieve more adequate behavior, counseling should first be concerned with helping him define, understand, and accept his current status. To help understand on-going behavior, interference theory provides a frame of reference in terms of four ideas.

The first is that people behave as they do because of various attitudes, assumptions, and beliefs they have about themselves. From these *assertions* an individual makes decisions about the feasibility of

---

[1] E. Lakin Phillips, "Introduction," in *Psychotherapy, A Modern Theory and Practice,* Prentice-Hall, 1956, p. xi.

[2] *Ibid.,* p. xvi.

[3] *Ibid.,* p. xvi.

various kinds of behavior. The adequacy of his behavior is largely a function of the validity of his assertions.

The second idea is that as an individual initiates behavior he observes its effects. This feedback to the individual can (to various degrees, obviously) either confirm or *disconfirm* his assertions.

The third idea is that when assertions are disconfirmed, *tensions* result which inhibit the reappraisal of assertions.

Fourth, because of the inflexibility and rigidity resulting from tensions, the individual strives harder to confirm initial assertions. Such behavior is described as *redundancy.*

What happens with the troubled individual, then, is that he involves himself in circular efforts to solve his problems. The greater his assertive efforts, the more disconfirmation and tension, and thus the more redundant behavior.

On additional aspect of interference theory is useful in developing a frame of reference for secondary school counselors, namely, *conflict.* To refer again to the decision-making construct, one of the major obstacles in making a decision even when uncertainty is reduced to its minimum is the conflict between positive and negative features of a decision. Typically, decisions are complex, and more often than not an individual perceives both favorable and unfavorable aspects inherent in each of the several possible alternatives. Thus, even when the facts are known, ambiguity about one's values (also assertions) can result in tension-producing conflict which inhibits effective decision making.

The frame of reference for secondary school counseling can now be outlined as follows:

1. *Decision-making construct:* The psychological problems of adolescents can be seen as decision-making problems.
2. *Conflict:* These decision-making problems almost always involve some conflict, either because of factual or emotional ambiguities or both.
3. *Assertions:* Behavior is a result of the assumptions, beliefs, and attitudes that one has about himself, others, and the world in which he lives.
4. *Disconfirmations:* The effects of behavior following decisions are fed back to the individual perceived, and they confirm or disconfirm assertion to varying degrees.
5. *Tension:* When assertions are disconfirmed, tensions result.

6. *Redundancy:* Tensions inhibit the ability of an individual to re-examine his assertions and to attempt to confirm them, and thus they cause redundant behavior.

It may be helpful now to view the frame of reference as applied to the case of Barbara, the student referred to earlier. The illustration of the decision-making construct need not be repeated. The remaining five aspects of the frame of reference can be illustrated as follows:

*Assertions:* Barbara's expectations of leadership positions and status were high. She believed herself to be capable and worthy of these, and she could accept nothing less.

*Disconfirmations:* Her peers, however, were unwilling to grant her automatic leadership and status. She perceived their resentment of her attempts to confirm her assertions, and their rejection of her as a person.

*Tension:* The barrage of resentment and lack of peer acceptance met by Barbara served to create tensions manifested in irritability.

*Redundancy:* The constant rebuffs from peers and the resulting tension made Barbara's behavior less flexible, and her persistent ineffective efforts to gain leadership and status became redundant attempts to confirm assertions.

The *conflicts* which developed, and which Barbara was increasingly able to define as counseling progressed, were centered in compromising her beliefs about her abilities with her desire for peer acceptance. Gaining peer acceptance seemed to require inhibition of her attempts to confirm assertions. Maintaining her assertions, on the other hand, seemed to entail continued rejection by peers and thus unhappiness.

## SUMMARY

In this chapter we have suggested that secondary school counseling needs a meaningful, realistic, practical frame of reference consistent with the short-term nature of school counseling. Accordingly, a nondepth frame of reference, taken in part from E. Lakin Phillips' interference theory, has been suggested and discussed. The frame of reference will be referred to throughout the remainder of the book.

## Suggested References

Bordin, Edward S., "An Analysis of Theories," in *Psychological Counseling*, Appleton-Century-Crofts, 1955, chap. 4.

Professor Bordin's analysis is based not so much on specific theories as on basic ways of perceiving human behavior and the implications of these ways for counseling practice. For this reason his discussions are very helpful and refreshing. One gets a glimpse of the forest instead of the trees.

Bross, I. D. J., *Design for Decision*, Macmillan, 1953.

A relatively nontechnical application of decision-making theory, with many implications for counseling.

Harper, Robert A., *Psychoanalysis and Psychotherapy, 36 Systems*, Prentice-Hall, 1959.

Brief descriptions of systems of counseling offer the student an abstract but meaningful overview of counseling thought from Freud to the present.

Phillips, E. Lakin, *Psychotherapy, A Modern Theory and Practice*, Prentice-Hall, 1956.

Although all of this book is highly recommended, high school counselors may be particularly interested in the Introduction; Chapter 1, "Interference Theory—Examples of Therapy"; Chapter 3, "Is the Concept of the Unconscious Necessary"; and Chapter 7, "Psychotherapy as Communicative Act." Phillips also includes three interview protocols illustrating his ideas.

....................................................................

# Some Aspects of Communication

---

Counselors need to remind themselves continually that counseling is above all else a specialized kind of communication. Thus, a counselor's effectiveness is in large part a function of his communication skills. This is not to say that he should necessarily possess a glib tongue, have a high verbal output, be persuasive, or show many of the other characteristics commonly associated with effective communication. Such attributes are certainly desirable, and may add to one's counseling effectiveness, but they are only of secondary importance. The kinds of communication skills that are basic to counseling place the greatest emphasis on listening. The idea that it is probably more difficult to become an effective listener than an effective talker is not a new one. It is particularly valid as applied to communication within the counseling interview. Thus, in preparation for the three chapters immediately following this one, which are devoted to various procedures of counseling, it will be helpful to discuss several aspects of communication that are basic to specific counseling procedures. These are taken up in this chapter in the following order: General Semantics and Communication, General Semantics and Adjustment, Nonverbal Communication, and Feedback in Counseling.

Volumes have been devoted to each of these topics, and the reader is referred to these for more adequate treatments. The brief discussions which follow are intended simply to point up the importance of each topic to counseling, and if possible, to motivate the student to pursue their study in greater detail.

## GENERAL SEMANTICS AND COMMUNICATION

The basic work in general semantics is *Science and Sanity* by Alfred Korzybski. Several writers have applied and expanded Korzybski's notions within the context of several particular applications. Certainly one of the most effective of these has been Wendell Johnson at the State University of Iowa. He has published several volumes dealing with general semantics. *People in Quandaries* was the first, and, for our purposes, the most relevant. The concepts touched on here are given thorough consideration in that volume.

What is general semantics? Perhaps the most effective answer to this question begins with an illustration rather than a definition. Consider the following autobiographical statement of an individual about 25 years old.

Asthma, when [I was] a small child, caused the family to move from our Oakland home to Los Angeles, where there were no further complications. There have been no other serious illnesses or disorders. Physical development has been normal, if a bit precocious.

Having been in attendance in an Oakland kindergarten for four months, the family's move to Los Angeles was an upsetting occurrence to me as a child of four for our new community had no kindergarten facilities. My mother appealed to the principal, and I was allowed to enter first grade, though only four years, six months old. Somewhere along the way, in fourth grade, I believe, I neglected to grasp basic principles of mathematics, and have suffered from this handicap since. Only recently, under the patient tutoring of a "quantitatively-minded" husband have some of the veiled mysteries surrounding a number of mathematical concepts been swept away. I feel I memorize easily and have an adequate retention period. My graduate work in education and psychology have proven the most stimulating of any studies undertaken before, and I am most eager to become more closely associated with the field of guidance.

I feel that I am relatively a stable person, with few periods of either extreme depression or elation. I attempt to at least recognize adjustment mechanisms within my behavior, and am satisfactorily able to resolve problems independently with a minimum of anxiety.

The demands of the doctoral curriculum in which my husband is engaged limit the social activities in which we can take part. We enjoy entertaining in our home, and although our eight months in the area has not developed a great number of intimates, we have a roster of interesting friends, whom we see, I am afraid, less often than we would like. Intra-family-wise, my marriage is a happy and satisfying one.

Besides my interest in art, which is now my vocation as well, I have set for myself the task of reading a number of the classics of literature, which have somehow been neglected along the collegiate way. A recent stay in Europe revealed a number of weaknesses in my background of knowledge of European writers and philosophers. The trip, by the way, sharpened our taste for travel and our desire to know intimately and comfortably a foreign language or two, and our hope to some day spend a year or two in study abroad. I have a seaman's navigation license, and occasionally sail for recreation; I have a great desire to own fine paintings, someday, and am building on a library in both

English and Spanish. As to influences, my father, now deceased, is probably responsible for my interests in the arts and in travel, for they were his loves and I was an only daughter.

I find myself in art, not because of any preconceived ambition to make a career in this field, but because it was the line of least resistance, for I received several scholarships, and was told I was talented. I enjoyed my studies, but was not and am not sufficiently excited about my work for it to be a satisfying experience. I very much enjoy working with people, especially young people and children. I enjoy the more academic life and think I will find research stimulating and from these work preferences have decided that the field of guidance and counseling psychology offers a rewarding future.

Assume now that you are an employer looking for a person to fill an important job. You want to know as much as possible about your several applicants, and you hope that the applicants' autobiographical statements will provide you with pertinent information. Ultimately, it is not specific information that you are after or will recall and use. What you most probably want is a composite picture or impression of each applicant. That is, you want to develop an abstraction from the information given. Your abstract will be based not only on the "pure information" provided, but will also be contaminated by the manner in which it is presented, and by your own experience, intelligence, and attitudes.

To illustrate the formation of such an abstract, advanced graduate students in personnel psychology were asked to read the autobiography printed above, playing the role of an employer. They were then asked to write a paragraph answering the question, "What kind of a person is this?" The four responses are listed below. It is suggested that before reading these you jot down your own response to that question.

1. The subject is highly verbal, intelligent, socially oriented, interested in art, literature, people, ideas, and other feminine-type activities. She probably has a tendency to gain satisfaction from social relationships, possible tendency to impress others, seems to have at least moderate self-insight, more adept at verbal skills than numerical ones, and may have some trouble relating to others (only child).

2. The person possibly had some illness during childhood which caused her to be more interested in intellectual pursuits rather than physical activities. She seems to have interests in fields (literature and art) which are somewhat typical of female interests. She probably is a fairly sensitive person, and perhaps her adjustment, though not poor, probably leaves something to be desired. It seems she and her husband have a fairly compatible married life. She might, however, be prone to becoming too involved in other people's problems, and tend to give advice rather than assume a more nondirective role.

3. A fairly well-adjusted, fairly ambitious, young matron with all the socially acceptable middle-class attitudes and values on education, the family, and society in general.

4. During childhood this individual had trying times. But as years passed, people became interested in this person and helped *him* to develop physically and mentally. His college experience has been the most enlightening and now *he* is happily married and has children. *He* will make creative contributions in *his* field of endeavor.

You may be thinking that we got what we asked for—that is, our method was so subjective that we could expect little else. Before discussing the results, then, examine Table 1, which gives the response frequencies of seven other graduate students in personnel work who read the autobiography and then completed an adjective check list to secure a more objective description of the individual in question.

The accuracy of the estimates made is not the concern here. Rather, the important point is the variability among the responses. In the four paragraph responses, this is obvious. Let us give them a somewhat categorical examination. First, consider the factual variance. Respondent 4 varies in terms of the subject's sex and family structure. Second, consider the general orientation of the four respondents. Each was given the same stimulus, but 1 responded primarily in terms of personal characteristics, 2 in terms of personal adjustment and vocational counselor behavior, 3 in terms of social normality, and 4 primarily in developmental terms. A third source of variance is observable, namely, the certainty with which the four raters responded. Respondents 1 and 2 reveal a relatively minor awareness of uncertainty, whereas responses 3 and 4 are much more cautious and tentative.

The data given in Table 1 reveal even greater variability of response. If, for the sake of comparison, scores of 3, 2, 1, and 0 are assigned to the four respective categories of response (i.e., very applicable equals 3, somewhat applicable equals 2, and so on), it can be determined that the total scores for the seven raters are as follows: 16, 20, 20, 35, 35, 38, 65. Yet each rater was read exactly the same information at the same time. Note, too, that all but five of the twenty-five adjectives received at least three out of four possible responses.

The phenomenon just illustrated is an obvious one—perhaps so obvious that it often escapes notice. Language and the things which language describes are not the same. Between the thing and the language is a selective perception involving a complexity of attitudes, biases, intelligence, knowledge, and motivations. The complexity of conditions is unique for each individual; thus, the language used to describe or identify the thing observed has to some degree a different meaning for each person. When a student says to a counselor, for

TABLE 1. Cumulative Responses of Seven Raters to an Adjective Check List Applied to a Student Autobiographical Statement

| Adjectives | Frequencies | | | |
| --- | --- | --- | --- | --- |
| | Very Applicable | Somewhat Applicable | Very Little If Any Applicability | Insufficient Information for a Judgment |
| Honest | 2 | 4 | 0 | 1 |
| Personable | 2 | 2 | 0 | 3 |
| Oversensitive | 2 | 1 | 3 | 1 |
| Intelligent | 4 | 2 | 1 | 0 |
| Sly | 0 | 2 | 2 | 3 |
| Defensive | 1 | 2 | 4 | 0 |
| Sincere | 2 | 3 | 1 | 1 |
| Resentful | 0 | 2 | 2 | 3 |
| Opportunist | 1 | 1 | 3 | 2 |
| Altruistic | 0 | 4 | 2 | 1 |
| Ambitious | 0 | 6 | 1 | 0 |
| Healthy | 3 | 2 | 0 | 2 |
| Kind | 1 | 2 | 0 | 4 |
| Neat | 0 | 0 | 0 | 7 |
| Careless | 0 | 0 | 1 | 6 |
| Organized | 0 | 3 | 2 | 2 |
| Purposeful | 2 | 2 | 3 | 0 |
| Naïve | 0 | 2 | 2 | 3 |
| Humorous | 0 | 1 | 0 | 6 |
| Resourceful | 0 | 4 | 2 | 1 |
| Ordinary | 0 | 1 | 4 | 2 |
| Confused | 1 | 3 | 3 | 0 |
| Emotional | 1 | 2 | 2 | 2 |
| Religious | 0 | 0 | 1 | 6 |
| Leader | 0 | 1 | 2 | 4 |

example, "I'm worried because my parents argue a lot," the initial meaning given to the statement by the counselor will probably be more a reflection of the counselor's personality and experience than the counselee's.

Even if we are aware of the phenomenon just illustrated, many of us continue to behave as if our impressions and interpretations of occurrences were in relatively general agreement with those of our associates. In other words, we make a great many assumptions about other people which are not warranted. "You cannot argue with facts," the saying goes, and we are invariably surprised, and often very much upset, when we discover that someone else didn't get the facts straight. How often, after "looking at the record," do individuals (of every level of intelligence and education) conclude their discussions with upset stomachs, verbal battles, fist fights, and, occasionally, homicides and suicides? In other words, the acts and means of communication have an important influence on the subject or content of the communication. What has all this to do with general semantics and counseling? The following section provides a partial answer.

Johnson summarizes the basis and function of general semantics as follows:

General semantics can be regarded as a systematic attempt to formulate the general method of science in such a way that it might be applied not only in a few restricted areas of human experience, but generally in daily life. It is concerned with science not as specialized laboratory techniques, not science as it depends upon highly refined precision apparatus, not science in the form of esoteric theories concerning the moons of Jupiter or the chemical composition of spot removers, not science as compilations of facts and statistics with regard to everything from wind velocities to petroleum—not science as technology—but science as a general method, as a basic orientation, as a generalized way of solving problems—and with due regard for the language of science; it is science in such a sense with which general semantics is concerned.[1]

General semantics, is, for our purposes, a method for increasing the effectiveness of human behavior. This is done primarily by (1) recognizing the relationships between words and what words stand for, and (2) providing some aids, in terms of method, for making these relationships facilitate, rather than inhibit, our behavior.

To say that the application of general semantics (science) will result in eliminating the affective part of human behavior is incorrect. The objectivity suggested by recognition of what words stand for in no way implies a coldness and mechanization of human interaction. On the contrary, the aim of general semantics is to facilitate warm, sensitive, and pleasant human interactions. Its basic premise is that these ends cannot be achieved amid verbal confusion and unnecessary am-

[1] Wendell Johnson, *People in Quandaries,* Harper, 1944, p. 33.

biguity. To be objective, in the present context, simply means to say what we mean and mean what we say, and to recognize that because of the nature of language a complete realization of this goal is impossible. It is impossible for several reasons, two of which are particularly important. The first is that our language is relatively rigid or static, whereas what language stands for, the world of facts, is extremely dynamic. Language is a compromise, a set of categories designed to facilitate abstraction. Language is discrete in nature, while the things that language symbolizes are continuous. Thus, one is not an exact image of the other. There are many opportunities for distortion and ambiguity; as a matter of fact, we can expect of language, by definition, a certain amount of ambiguity. The amount or extent of ambiguity, however, depends partly on the extent to which we recognize the relation of language to fact and the extent to which we operate in the light of this relation.

The second reason why it is impossible to say what we mean, and to mean what we say, follows from the first. It has to do with the abstract nature of language. "John went to town," of course, does not tell the whole story—far from it; we assume that it represents the essential fact of a series of circumstances concerning John. It may, in fact, do this. That is, the sentence may very well serve to communicate between the "sayer" and the "hearer" the important fact of the matter. But again, it may not. The sentence tells us little about place, time, motive, or events which may have happened along the way. Nevertheless, the sentence may be satisfactory to us because of various *assumptions* which we make about it. In other words, we go beyond what was actually said and infer details of particular interest to us.

Obviously, abstraction as a characteristic of language is desirable and necessary. There is often no point in reporting every detail of a situation which we can recall. Indeed, an overconcern with details of description is frequently boring, painful, or even somewhat pathological. The man who continually relates the minute details of his vacation trip to his fellow workers ruins what could be a brief, informative verbal experience for his listeners. The teacher who forces his students to memorize the birthdays and wedding dates of every captain and colonel in the Civil War inhibits real learning for his students, and the lady who insists on making a full-length novel out of her child's first day in school may find herself abandoned by all of her friends.

Abstracting causes difficulties in two ways. The first, which has been implied, is that people sometimes fail to recognize that they are abstracting; the second source of difficulty arises from a breakdown of the abstracting process itself. Johnson has coined the phrase "short-circuited abstracting" to account for this breakdown in the process. Essentially, what happens is that we accept an inference as a fact and proceed to build further inferences, that is, to move to higher levels of abstraction, on the basis of the untested inference. If the inference is not valid, or as is quite often the case, is only partially valid, then the behavior based on our final abstractions may be considerably inappropriate. An example may clarify this point:

A student wanted to become a computing machine technician. His counselor felt that this was an inappropriate vocational choice because the boy had a deformed arm. When talking with the student and his parents, the counselor raised this question and suggested that the deformity would be a handicap placing definite limits on the student's ability to achieve in the chosen vocation. The boy and his parents accepted this idea and consequently all concerned automatically excluded all manipulatory occupations from career-planning considerations. They inferred the condition to be a handicap and behaved as if the inference were a fact.

In this particular case, the real fact of the matter was that the nature of the deformity and the boy's attitude towards it in no way presented a handicap in the chosen occupation. However, the boy spent nearly two confused and unhappy years in college preparing to become a mathematics teacher before a counselor helped him to test his *inference* against facts rather than against other inferences. Available occupational literature plus a visit to a local business machine office provided evidence to invalidate the inference.

Thus far, we have been discussing the first application of general semantics to counseling, namely, a recognition of the relationships between words and what words stand for. With this admittedly scanty discussion as a background, we turn to the second application of general semantics to counseling, that of providing methods of making these relationships facilitate rather than inhibit our behavior.

## GENERAL SEMANTICS AND ADJUSTMENT

Our basic premise, simplified and rephrased, is that problems encountered in counseling are very often partially bound up in the language that counselees use to describe their difficulties. For example, when a student makes the assertion, "This is just about the most useless course that I've ever taken," and requests that he be allowed to drop that course, what is he really saying about himself and the course? The following list gives only a few of the statements which may be more accurate descriptions of his problem.

1. I just flunked a test.
2. I didn't finish my assignment for today.
3. The teacher wouldn't excuse me for a baseball trip.
4. I can't understand the textbook.
5. The room is too hot and stuffy.
6. The teacher has several mannerisms which irritate me.
7. My dad forced me to take this course.
8. The course seems unrelated to my vocational goal.
9. The course does not cover the material I was told it would cover.
10. I've already read all of the course content in other courses.

Not infrequently, helping the student clarify the statement of his felt problem is a satisfactory solution in itself. The following interview excerpt serves to illustrate this point further.

C: Lately, then, you have become concerned about college again?
S: Yes, I had it all figured out last year, but now, I don't know. I thought I had the ability, but now, as I have to decide on one college, I think maybe I can't make it.
C: You are again questioning your ability to do college work?
S: Yes, partly, I think. What I really mean is that I don't know any more whether or not I should go to college. Maybe I don't have the right kind of personality for uh—well to live in a dorm with lots of other people. It's sort of discouraging, since I thought I had it all figured out once; and I really worry a lot about whether or not I should go to college. Sometimes I can't get my mind off of it.

What is this student's problem? This should be a pretty easy question to answer, if we take what is said as representing what is meant. But can we? The problem, as stated and, according to the counselor's initial perception, is something like this: "In terms of my ability and personality, I don't know whether I can succeed at college."

Let us apply the question, "What do you mean?" to the problem as stated. (Let it be emphasized that we are not in search of depth interpretations, hidden meanings, repressed desires, or the like. We are simply asking that the problem be stated in more precise, less abstract terms, and that inferences be recognized as such.) For example, the counselor might begin by asking the student, "What do you mean by college?" or "Is attending college A exactly the same as attending college B?" Obviously, it is not. Helping the student recognize this should make his basic questions more meaningful, and thus somewhat more answerable. The counselor could also raise the questions, "What do you mean by success?" or "What do you mean by good grades and making it at college?" For example, is the student thinking in terms of a rather arbitrary dichotomy? Does he see one as either succeeding or failing in college? If he does, wouldn't it help if he could realize that success and failure, and thus "making it," and "not making it," represent the two extreme ends of a continuum? Actually, there are probably two questions to be considered, the first being what the student's chances for persisting in college A are, and the second, what his personal standards of adequacy are. Elaborating the second question, is a C average, though sufficient for persistence in college, satisfactory to him, or does he, in terms of his standards, need to be more than a C student? And in regard to the first question, what kinds of chances is he willing to take? What do the odds on his persistence in college have to be before he is willing to enroll in college A? In other words, what does he mean by "know" when he says, "I don't know whether I can succeed"?

It is also important to ask, "What do you mean, should I go to college?" Does he mean, as we have been assuming so far, "What are my chances for success?" or does he really mean, "Will it give me the status, added vocational training, job-getting ability, and other advantages I want?" Or does he mean, "Will it please my parents more if I attend and flunk out than if I don't attend at all?" Or is he asking, "Am I willing to accept the probable loss of peer and family status entailed in not attending?"

Obviously, there are other "What do you mean?" questions which could be asked about this illustrative problem, but these examples should suffice. The student in the illustration undoubtedly has some "real" problems, that is, some important decisions to make. But until he understands what his alternatives are and what they entail, he stands little chance of making meaningful and effective choices. It follows that until he understands the limitations of the language by which he has described his problems, he cannot hope to perceive the alternatives and what they entail. In other words, part of his problem is the language he is using to describe it.

There is another type of question which is useful in helping students solve their problems: namely, "How do you know?" As we have seen, by answering the question, "What do you mean?" both the counselee and the counselor may come to better understanding of the relevant assertions. Given this understanding, then, it is helpful to apply the question, "How do you know?" The student in the example expressed uncertainty about the extent to which his "personality" would allow him to "fit into dorm life." The interview continued in the following way:

C: Can you tell me a little more about what you mean by your personality not letting you fit into dorm life?

S: Well, I don't know. I guess I just don't know whether I would like to live in a dorm with other people. (*Pause.*) I think there might be too much noise, and it would be hard to study.

C: You feel dorm life might interfere with your studying?

S: Well, sort of. Actually, it's more than that. I mean I visited a friend of mine at college earlier this year and spent the week end in his dorm. That's what started my worrying. I just don't think that I would like it. (*Pause.*)

C: Can you tell me more about your experience?

S: Yes. In the first place there was a lot of drinking there. I don't drink, and I don't think underage kids should. Anyway, even if they do, I don't. I think my friend and his friends thought I was funny, kind of sissy—you know—not one of the fellows—because I wouldn't drink. They got me a date, a blind date, and we all went to a dance. I don't dance very well, but I went along. It was really disgusting. Some of the girls had been drinking, too. Well, anyway, I don't think that's any way for college people to act. They weren't even 21 yet, and if that's what going to college is like—I know that this was a week end and all, but still. You know—I just don't want to be that way, and if I went to college I would probably be very unhappy.

C: You feel that because you have different standards than most college students, you would be uncomfortable at college?

S: Yes. (*Pause.*)

C: You were also a little disappointed in your friend's behavior?

S: Yes, I thought he was like I am. He used to be, but now he's just like all college students.

C: You were unhappy because you felt he has lowered his moral standards since he went to college?

S: I really was.

C: Does your friend seem different in this respect when he is home—I mean does he drink and carouse around?

S: Well, that's not fair. He doesn't drink all the time—he really had only one drink that night at college. Maybe I overemphasized that part of it.

C: Perhaps it wasn't so much the drinking, but the new people and the new situation that was uncomfortable to you.

S: You may be right.

C:  It's often difficult to be comfortable and have a good time the first time you meet people, isn't it?

S:  Yes, I think so. Maybe that was it. I still don't like the drinking, but no one was drunk. I'm not even sure that some of them had been drinking. They just acted different. I mean, I felt kind of lost the whole week end— like not knowing what to do next, and no one paid much attention to me.

This excerpt illustrates the importance of asking "How do you know?" The student in the example was making certain assertions about himself, about college life, and about the relationship between the two. What the counselor was attempting to do was to help the counselee recognize these. The counselor began to help the student check the validity of his assertions by encouraging an examination of the evidence upon which they were based.

As he is able to restate his problem in more precise, meaningful, and accurate terms, thus perceiving the semantical limitations and ambiguities surrounding it, he will be in a much better position to deal with its nonlanguage aspects. By examining the validity of his inferences, the student also can achieve better understanding of the language with which he describes his problems. With more adequate understanding of the validity of his assertions, and acceptance of the re-evaluation, he finds that the way to working with the nonlanguage aspects of the problem is much clearer. That is, once he recognizes, understands, and accepts his assertions, and then checks their validity, his problem becomes meaningful and solvable. Often, as a matter of fact, it is then partially solved.

To summarize, it has been suggested that general semantics can be employed as an aid or tool in helping students to define and understand their problems. In this sense, general semantics does not provide any answers, except in the sense that when assertions are stated in meaningful terms, the student often is able immediately to reject them as invalid. What general semantics does provide, in the present sense, are questions or assertions stated in terms which permit validation. When "I cannot succeed at college" is restated as, for example, "The chances for my maintaining passing grades at college A are too poor for me to risk my status," the student has made significant progress towards solving his problem.

## NONVERBAL COMMUNICATION IN COUNSELING

It would be interesting to know the proportion of face-to-face communication between normal individuals that is of a nonverbal nature. The securing of such data would be tremendously complex, but the very contemplation of how such a study might be designed suggests that we often fail to recognize the importance of nonverbal aspects of communication.

Talking about nonverbal behavior is a little like talking about a musical performance. One can describe it to others in great detail, and point out exactly what to listen for, but the description will fall short of adequate communication until the other has actually listened to the performance. Describing nonverbal phenomena in words also falls short of adequate communication. Thus, the purpose of this section is to emphasize the need for counselors to be perceptive of nonverbal signs from counselees, and to make several suggestions on how this might be accomplished. The perceptive skills in this area are left, as they must be for the most part, for each counselor to develop.

While nonverbal communication in itself can be extremely effective, as, for example, with deaf-mutes, and also with normal individuals in certain traumatic situations, its primary importance to counseling is its influence on verbal communication. Counseling practicum situations provide an excellent illustration of this point. An almost standard procedure in practicums is for the instructor and the practicum-counselor to discuss tape recordings of counseling sessions that the counselor has made. Almost invariably in these critique sessions, the practicum counselor will take issue with some observation or suggestion made by the instructor. For example, in response to an instructor's suggestion that the counselor pursued a topic which the counselee said was not important, the counselor might respond, "He said he wasn't worried, but the expression on his face led me to believe that he was," or "He didn't say anything, but his posture suggested that the matter was something which he wanted to discuss, but couldn't bring himself to mention."

The author's experience with a typical practicum group, confirms the point. The students met as a group each week to discuss a particular interview recorded by one of the group members. Frequently, about half of the group had observed the interview by means of one-way window facilities, whereas the remainder of the group had only listened to a tape recording of the session. From the comments made, it became possible to predict with considerable accuracy which students had observed the interview. The listeners, perceiving only verbal communication and thus not being aware of the nonverbal aspect of the interview, responded only in terms of verbal content. Many of their comments apparently lacked validity in the perception of those who were cognizant of the nonverbal aspects of the interview. Similarly, the observers tended to make more penetrating and subtle comments than the listeners, thus, in the writer's opinion, often manifesting their awareness of the influence of nonverbal signs.

The point need not be labored. Almost everyone has observed the phenomenon in various situations. The logical question would seem to be, "What can counselors do to become more perceptive of nonverbal communication?" Are there rules or methods for systematically taking account of the nonverbal aspects of counseling interviews? Perhaps the question can be answered in part by a brief consideration of some of the nonverbal signs that are used and what happens when one attempts to derive meaning from them.

First, what are the types of signs? Most of us could agree that facial expressions, bodily gestures, nervous mannerisms, and general posture are typical means of communicating feeling or thought. For example, a smile or a grimace may indicate that a counselee means just the opposite of what he says. The student who grimaces as he says, "Sure, I'm happy with school," may be speaking facetiously. The counselee who makes an assertion in a very calm and natural voice, but who makes some gross bodily movement at the same time, may be indicating that he is not at all certain that what he is saying about himself is true. Drumming on the table, pulling an ear, wringing one's hands, and the like can suggest an emotional concern not at all evident in the verbal communication of a counselee. General posture can suggest moods, self-estimates, embarrassment, and other attitudes. As a matter of fact, such behavior is so common that many of us tend to operate according to nonverbal sign stereotypes which we develop. Often we modify our stereotypes in the light of the verbal content of a given situation, thus making them seem valid to us, but, nevertheless, they are still stereotypes.

The faith placed in these stereotypes as a means of interpreting nonverbal signs is rather astounding, at least in view of the little that is known about their communicative validity and the inadequate theoretical foundation upon which they are based. The reader who has examined company manuals on sales technique, or who has taken a company in-service sales course, is very likely to be aware of this. In these sources, descriptions and even classifications of various kinds of nonverbal signs are often given. A very presumptuous discussion of this sort was included in a manual prepared for an encyclopedia sales company by an industrial psychology firm. After the initial sales pitch had been described verbatim, the sales trainee was given a choice of four or five "closes." The decision as to which close should be employed in specific cases was to depend on the extent to which the prospective customer had been sold—which, in turn, was to be determined by the expression on his face at the completion of the main part of the sales pitch. If he looked eager, closing 1 should be employed; if he looked doubtful, closing 2; if he looked resentful, closing 3, and so on. Incidentally, the company had an extremely successful sales record, but this was primarily due to the high quality of the product and an effective national advertising program. As a matter of fact, it is probable that a significant negative relationship existed between the sales volume of individual salesmen and the extent to which the rules on nonverbal clues were followed.

This illustration is merely an exaggeration of the kind of stereotyping of nonverbal signs many of us are guilty of in everyday communication.

It is particularly important that the counselor avoid stereotypes in his reactions to the counselee during the counseling session. Just as the counselor is attentive to the unique quality of the counselee as an individual as shown in words, he should also be attentive to the individual counselee's nonverbal communication.

To reiterate, counselors should strive diligently to utilize nonverbal aspects of communication as means of achieving more complete understanding of the facts and feelings that counselees attempt to communicate. In doing this, the counselor can perceive nonverbal signs in two ways. To use academic terminology, he can seek to understand nonverbal signs normatively and idiographically. In the writer's opinion, the existing evidence on nonverbal signs does not suggest that the counselor can make valid and reliable normative inferences from them. What he can more realistically strive to achieve is to make idiographic sense out of nonverbal signs. What one actually observes are nonverbal signs of a given counselee during a counseling contact, or a series of them. It is the change in nonverbal signs and the total patterns of nonverbal signs, viewed in terms of how they are used and what they mean for a particular counselee, that can be meaningful. Obviously, nonverbal signs have no inherent meanings. They are learned, as all language is learned, but, because they are much less systematized than formal language, only very limited assumptions about their common usage can be made. Traditional language can be characterized as a system of symbols with more or less common meaning to all those who have learned the system. Nonverbal communication, on the other hand, might be more accurately described as a system of signs which in great part is understood only by the individual. True, the number of signs, in a gross sense, are limited, and these are employed in some way by most individuals, but the system which gives them meaning is much more peculiar to the individual than a traditional language system can be.

Part of the counselor's task is to become familiar with the system or manner in which an individual employs nonverbal signs in conjunction with his verbal language. Thus, as the counselor observes a counselee employ various nonverbal signs, they begin to have more precise meaning. For example, a counselee grimaces when he means to understate a point, or he wrings his hands when he is discussing areas of important conflict, or he tips his chair back and talks in a louder voice when he refers to accomplishments which seem to disconfirm his basic assertions. A pattern develops, and perhaps as counseling progresses, the changes in the pattern are perceived to be concomitant with verbally expressed changes in attitude and self-knowledge. The counselee's nonverbal signs begin to add sense to what he is saying as they are observed and compared with other things which he says and does. But when the next counselee comes in and leans back in his chair, it may or may not be a sign of uncertainty. Perhaps his back hurts—or the chair is uncomfortable (as is the case with counselee chairs in most school counseling offices). The point is that the only legitimate means of making sense out of a particular counselee's nonverbal communication is in an idiographic sense. It is understandable in terms of his other behavior, not in terms of the behavior of others.

## FEEDBACK IN COUNSELING

In the following chapters, frequent references will be made to the concept of feedback. A brief discussion of feedback as an important aspect of communication in counseling should make what follows more meaningful. While the concept of feedback is certainly not new, its well-defined and systematic application is a relatively recent development.

As theoretical papers concerned with communication were published, various fields of applied science began to employ communication theory ideas in a variety of situations. The concept of feedback, basic to communication theory, has had particularly wide and varied application. This is because, to some degree, almost everything that we do is based on a prediction. Therefore, before repeating an action, one needs some indication of the success of the prediction. Consider, for example, the very simple illustration of a man shooting a rifle in a shooting gallery. He aims the rifle at the target and predicts that if his aim is correct he will hit the target and a bell will ring. The sound of the bell, or the absence of it, is an illustration of feedback. The ringing of the bell is information fed back to the man; it indicates to him that he hit the target, and gives him some assurance that his aiming and firing procedures were appropriate. The bell's failure to ring also represents feedback information, but in this case indicates that his aim and firing procedures were not appropriate (assuming, of course, that the gun was loaded and in firing condition). However, in this simple illustration, a man in the latter situation has received only a gross kind of feedback. He has no means of knowing in which direction to correct his aim, for example. A soldier on a military firing range provides a more complex illustration of feedback. After he aims and fires at his target, an observer indicates not only whether he hit or missed it, but also the degree and accuracy of direction, thus allowing the soldier to correct his aim with purpose. He fires a second time and more information is fed back to him, and so the process continues.

While the last example above represents an effective use of feedback, it is extremely simple, in that only one procedure and one objective are involved. An example of the extremely sophisticated use of feedback, employing a multitude of interrelated procedures and objectives, is provided by guided missiles and rockets. Whereas a rifle is fired and observations made of what happens, the missile is launched in terms of predicted conditions and events, and then data on the actual conditions are fed back to computing machines. These almost instantaneously use the feedback to make new predictions, which, in turn, immediately initiate changes in the operation of the missile, the effects of which changes are fed back to the computers. In addition, of course, vast and complex amounts of feedback data are preserved, and these facilitate further developments and refinements in future missiles. Without a systematic attempt to obtain feedback data, scientists could test only the most gross predictions. Systematic feedback provides a means for effective behavior.

Most uses of feedback are at levels of complexity and sophistication falling somewhere between the two extremes illustrated above. For example, when you start out in your car for your first trip between San Francisco and Las Vegas, you would do well to prepare for the trip by spending some time studying a road map (and, incidentally, your bank book). You would, in a sense, identify various landmarks along the way which could serve as progressive measures of the accuracy of your prediction. If, then, as you traveled past the point where you expected to observe the first landmark, it did not appear, you would probably restudy your map, or acquire information from a native, which would put you back on the appropriate route. In a very real sense, you would be securing feedback so as to maximize your chances for obtaining your objective in the manner most satisfactory to you.

Quite often, of course, our goals or objectives are not so well defined as in the last example, and further, procedures for obtaining them are not nearly so easily discernible. Like the first airplane pilots, one must fly by the seat of one's pants a great deal of the time. This is very frequently true for the counselor in a counseling session. It is not that counselors have no alternative but to stumble along with students, or that their helpfulness is mostly a matter of chance. Rather, if counselors are to utilize their competencies effectively, it is exceedingly important that they systematically attempt to obtain feedback from counselees. As suggested earlier, the counseling function is dependent on maximizing the meaningfulness of communication between the counselee and the counselor. To achieve this, the counselor must constantly be obtaining feedback from the counselee to determine if what he meant was what the counselee understood. He must also take the responsibility of providing feedback to the counselee, so that the counselee can estimate the extent to which he is making sense to the counselor. The importance of feedback and illustrations of it in counseling sessions will be discussed again in following chapters. To reiterate, the purpose here has been only to describe the concept by illustration, and to emphasize its importance to effective counseling.

## SUMMARY

As a closing note to this chapter, it is well to point out two things. First, as the chapter title suggests, only limited aspects of the processes of communication have been treated—and these very briefly. Attempting to discuss the many aspects of communication in greater detail would be unnecessary in view of the many excellent references available. The concepts discussed are those which have been found most useful in attempts to help others become more effective counselors. Second, it is important to remember that whereas the primary perspective used in this chapter has been that of counselees, most of what has been said is equally applicable to counselors. Specifically, the problems of verbal and nonverbal communication that are common among students, exist in some degree among even the most experienced and well-prepared counselors.

## Suggested References

*General Semantics*

Johnson, Wendell, *People in Quandaries, The Semantics of Personal Adjustment,* Harper, 1946.
    This highly readable volume presents and illustrates the concepts of general semantics.
Johnson, Wendell, *Your Most Enchanted Listener,* Harper, 1946.
    The art of listening is discussed from the perspective of general semantics.
Korzybski, Alfred, *Science and Sanity: An Introduction to Non-Aristotelian Systems and General Semantics,* 2nd ed., Science Press, 1941.
    The basic work in general semantics.
Rapaport, Anatole, *Operational Philosophy,* Harper, 1953.
    Although not concerned with counseling per se, this book can help the counselor take a critical look at his communication competencies.

*Communication*

Barbara, D. A., "The Value of Non-Verbal Communication in Personality Understanding," *Journal of Nervous and Mental Disease,* 1956, *123:*286–291.
Cronbach, L. J., "The Counselor's Problems from the Perspective of Communication Theory," in *New Perspectives in Counseling,* Vivian H. Hewer (ed.), University of Minnesota Press, 1955, pp. 3–19.
Ruesch, J., and W. Kees, *Nonverbal Communication,* Berkeley, University of California Press, 1956.
Wiener, Norbert, *Cybernetics: The Human Use of Human Beings,* Technology Press, 1949.
    The problems of communication and learning are discussed from a point of view different from that typical of counselors. A useful perspective of the communications process is thus provided.

# CHAPTER 4

## A General Perspective of the Counseling Interview

This chapter and the two which follow are concerned with the counseling process itself. A brief preview of the topics treated in these chapters should be helpful. Chapter 4 builds up a kind of ostensive definition of counseling—"kind of" because ideally the reader should be taken to a place where counseling was actually taking place and allowed to observe and discuss what he saw and heard. Obviously, we have to settle for something less. Thus, in this chapter typescripts of actual counseling interviews with secondary school students are presented and discussed, along with other illustrations of counseling functions.

Chapter 5 is devoted to a discussion of the techniques and procedures (that is, counseling skills) which the professional counselor employs. It is true that the heart of counseling is the counselor's understanding of and sensitivity to counselees, and that counseling techniques are of secondary importance. At the same time, if one were to question beginning (and even experienced) counselors about the things that prevent them from counseling more effectively, a majority of them would probably indicate that while they never completely understand students' problems, their greatest difficulty is in knowing what to do in counseling. That is, their counseling tools, so to speak, are inadequate. Now it is obvious that both greater understanding of students' problems and more effective counseling skills are in large part the outcome of counseling experience. Nevertheless (and this is the rationale for considering counseling techniques in themselves), without a basic set of skills to begin with, counseling experience is difficult to acquire. To begin a counseling career without these skills starts the counselor out on the wrong foot. He feels inadequate and uncomfortable in the counseling interview, and thus is likely to avoid the counseling functions of his job and concentrate on its less threatening aspects. On the other hand, if he has some notion of appropriate counseling skills he will feel more adequate and less uncomfortable, and thus be able to gain a measure of satisfaction in counseling from the start. With this kind of reinforcement he is likely to devote more time to counseling and consequently provide himself with an opportunity to develop greater understanding and skills.

In Chapter 6 a number of situations frequently encountered by secondary school counselors are discussed. The point is made here that knowing how to provide needed assistance in these situations is basic to effective secondary school counseling.

In short, the primary purpose of Chapters 4, 5, and 6 is to provide a notion of what happens, or should happen, when a counselor and a student sit down for a counseling session. What do you do that makes counseling with a student different from giving him advice or just talking to him?

## THE INTERVIEWS

The first two counseling interview typescripts presented below involve a ninth-grade boy who was initially seen because of low achievement in an algebra course. (The typescripts have been condensed in various places.)

FIRST INTERVIEW

1 C:  Could you tell me a little about why you feel you'd like to come in here?

2 S:  Well, I'd like to get better grades . . . get better grades and—um—I guess that's about all.

3 C:  What are some of the things that you can see that are keeping you from getting better grades?

4 S:  In my algebra I have an awfully hard time, but then I don't know why, especially in my tests. Cuz when I . . . I can usually do the problems at home on my homework, and then when I take the test then I just can't do them. I don't remember how to do them.

5 C:  You really know the stuff, but you can't come through on the tests with it?

6 S:  Yeah. And in my Latin, there it's—uh—I think Latin's quite easy, but I just got a test back today, a review test, they give us a review test every time we cover a certain number of lessons or something like that, and—

uh—I got a B in that. Latin's very easy; I got a . . . we have a vocabulary test where she gives certain words to memorize . . . in each lesson they have certain words written down and the meanings, and I memorize those, and the next day she gives us a quiz on them and I got an A in that. Latin is really for me very easy. And so is social studies, which is history right now. English is easy, too. The only really hard subject is algebra.

7 C:  So this is really what you're concerned about, your algebra grade. And yet you say you get the stuff . . . you can do the problems at home, but have trouble in the class.

8 S:  I listen to the teacher all the time. It just doesn't sink in.

9 C:  Have you had trouble with math generally before?

10 S:  Well, I haven't had any real trouble with math. It's been pretty easy.

11 C:  Well, this is a sort of new situation in algebra.

12 S:  I suppose really it shouldn't be hard because it's just—well, it's kind of like math, just letters and symbols instead of numbers.

13 C:  How do you feel about the course generally?

14 S:  Well, I like it; I like the teacher. It's awfully hard . . . (*Trails off.*)

15 C:  You're in your first term of algebra.

16 S:  Well—uh—this is my second semester.

17 C:  This is your second semester of the first year?

18 S:  Yeah.

19 C:  How did you do last term?

20 S:  Well, last term I . . . it was a little easier. This term it's awfully hard . . . harder . . .

21 C:  What grade did you get last term?

22 S:  Last term I think I got—uh—um . . . (*hesitates*) a D-plus. (*Seems reluctant to mention his grade.*)

23 C:  That's pretty disturbing to you, getting that low a grade . . . especially compared to the way you think you should do?

24 S:  Uh—yes, I should be doing better . . .

25 C:  The other courses are all pretty good, huh?

26 S:  Yes, they're all . . . I'm taking English, social studies, Latin, ROTC, and algebra. And study. They're all easy except the algebra.

27 C:  What sorts of grades do you get in the other subjects?

28 S:  Well, I get pretty good grades. I know that I probably got a B in English last time, C in Latin and social studies. I think I've worked harder in Latin and social studies. And in algebra I got an F. That was very upsetting because it was the first F I ever got.

29 C:  Yeah, that'd be pretty tough.
(*Pause.*)

30 C:  When you get upset by a grade like this, does this then—uh—make it harder for you to do better . . . make you try too hard almost?

31 S:  It does make it a little harder, seems to.
(*Pause.*)

32 C:  Can you put your finger on anything in algebra that makes it tougher than the other subjects?

33 S:  Well, no, I don't think I can. It's just hard all over.

34  C:   Um-hmm.

(*Pause.*)

35  C:   Are there pretty much the same people in your algebra class, other students, as in your other courses?

36  S:   Well, I think most of the kids that are in algebra are in my English and Latin classes. But—uh—let's see there's . . . one boy in my social studies class that's in algebra and that's all. In my other classes there are quite a few, especially English.

(*Pause.*)

37  C:   I'm trying to think of some way to approach this . . . Suppose you were to drop algebra . . .

38  S:   I was going to take it in summer school, but—uh . . .

39  C:   You think it would be easier to get in summer school?

40  S:   Well—uh, it would be easier—uh—do they let you take just one course in summer school?

41  C:   Yeah, I think so.

42  S:   Well, it might be then, then it might be a little easier if I could just concentrate on that, and wouldn't have anything else.

43  C:   You feel as though then it would be a matter of, or it is now a matter mostly of concentration. Not having the time to get to it.

44  S:   I could get it if I just didn't work all the time on it, but [. . . that's what he said . . .] but of course—uh . . .

45  C:   It just seems like one of those things that doesn't come easy?

46  S:   Yeah.

(*Pause.*)

47  C:   How does your family feel about it?

48  S:   Well, Mother of course wants me to do better, of course, for a grade, but she wants me to go to summer school and—uh . . .

(*Pause.*)

49  C:   Your mother feels as though you'd do better in summer school?

50  S:   Well, she's . . . she wants me to go to summer school and make it up this term.

51  C:   She doesn't want to see you getting behind then in school, is that it?

52  S:   Yeah.

(*Pause.*)

53  C:   This is kind of a blow to your pride, too, I imagine.

54  S:   That's the worst, seems like the worst part of it.

55  C:   Yeah, that's probably mainly what's the disturbing part of it.

56  S:   Yeah.

(The second half of the interview is more of the same—with many pauses, nothing introduced but the fact that he does not do well in algebra and is disturbed by it. The student, in general, was not very verbal. He seemed to want help with his problem, but was somehow unable to talk to the counselor about it.)

The counselor began this interview (after a brief conversation which is not included) by asking the student to tell about himself and his expectations from counseling. In terms of our frame of reference he was saying: What are your assertions? to what extent are they being confirmed? and what is the nature of the conflict, if any, which results from disconfirmation? For himself, the counselor was attempting to discover how appropriate the student's assertions were, to what extent he recognized them, what were the decisions that the student needed to make, and what could be done to facilitate his decision making.

What did the student say about himself; what was he asserting? Look, for example, at statements 4, 6, 8, 24, and 26. Wasn't the student asserting that he was relatively bright, at least was capable of adequate achievement in school? What, then, was his problem? Again in terms of our frame of reference, he was saying that his ability assertion was being disconfirmed in algebra. In other words, he was a good student, but he was having difficulty learning algebra. Actually, he did not quite admit to this. What he actually said was that he understood his assignments but did poorly on tests.

The counselor attempted to discover how the student felt about his difficulty, and what conflicts and tensions were produced by the disconfirmations (23, 28, 30). This particular counselor also attempted to discover any related problems which might have influenced the achievement situation (47). As the final note indicates, the remainder of the interview was relatively unproductive. The student seemed reluctant to discuss his feelings about the situation with the counselor.

The following counseling interview took place a week after the first one:

SECOND INTERVIEW

1 S:  Well, we had our algebra examination today. I did pretty well this time. However . . .

2 C:  It's still kind of rough though.

3 S:  Still rough. We had fifteen problems and I took the whole period just to get them done.

4 C:  This gets pretty discouraging.

5 S:  Um-hmm. Mother says she thinks maybe I just don't know how to study.

6 C:  So you suppose there's something in the way you should study for algebra that's different from the way you study for the other courses?

7 S:  Well, I do it the same way. Look at it and then . . . look at it and then try it out, then do the problems.

8 C:  Basically, you feel as though you have the ability, and your mother feels you do . . .

9 S:  Yes.

10 C: . . . so there must be something . . . some other thing like study habits.

11 S: Yeah.

12 C: How do you feel about this?

13 S: Well—uh—I think I should be getting better grades. Specially on tests which are my real downfall, of course.

14 C: Other than on the tests you do pretty well.

15 S: Yeah.

16 C: Adequately, anyway.

17 S: Yeah.

18 C: Well, there must be something about algebra that makes it harder than your other subjects.

19 S: Yeah, could be, about the only answer I can think of, really.

(*Pause.*)

20 C: Have you tried any other study methods, different ways of studying?

21 S: Well, I haven't really. I can't think of any others.

22 C: But you feel as though there must be some way you can get it, some way to get at it.

23 S: Um-hmm.

24 C: And the way you're doing just isn't doing it for you.

25 S: Uh-uh.

26 S: In Latin, when we have to learn vocabulary lessons, and we have to learn the words, and our teacher, you know, she—uh—gives us the Latin word and we write out which gender and—uh—it is and write out singular or plural if it's a noun and which gender it is, the definition, meaning, or if it's a verb, write the principal parts and meaning and things like that and I always write the word and the meanings over and over until I can give them. In algebra I write the problems out, and first I . . . on the page they have the sample problems, show how to do them, and I do that one, you know, do what it says, then I pick some different places on the page and, they come out, and then I take the test and I just can't remember what to do when I see it and how to do it, lots of times.

27 C: You can do them when you have an example in the book, but on the test, it's another story.

(*Pause.*)

28 C: It must be kind of a hopeless feeling after you study and study and . . .

29 S: It is.

30 C: And nothing you've tried has improved things.

31 S: No.

(*Pause.*)

32 C: Well, maybe it would help if we talked about ways we might help you here. Or what you see that we could do.

33 S: Well, uh . . . I don't really know . . .

34 C: It's kind of hard to really think of something.

35 S: Uh-huh.

(*Pause.*)

36 C: Well, up to now all we've talked about is just your algebra grades

and—uh . . . which is really your only problem . . . the only area in which you're having difficulty. And if by some way, either by changing your study methods, or maybe going to summer school to make up the algebra, if you could bring your grade up and not drop behind in your class you'd be in good shape.

37 S: Um-hmm.

(*Pause.*)

38 C: Well—uh—let me see how I can put this . . . outside the algebra class there really aren't any problems.

39 S: No, my Latin and English and social studies are easy, ROTC's easy, so . . .

40 C: So you're really only uncomfortable or disturbed in algebra.

41 S: Uh-huh.

42 C: Well—uh—so when you're outside algebra—uh—does this disturbance or difficulty carry over outside the algebra class into other areas? If you could just cut the algebra out of your life—uh—say the hour a day you spend in the algebra class, if that was just missing, you'd be perfectly happy then with the rest of it?

43 S: Yeah, cuz I like all my teachers and I don't have a hard time with my other courses, it's just the algebra.

44 C: Well what I'm trying to get at really is, and not doing it too well—uh—does this worry about algebra carry over into the other things you do? Do you worry about algebra outside algebra class?

45 S: Oh, I guess I do really. I can say I do.

46 C: Uh-huh. Well, does this have any effect on the other things you do, the way you feel about other things or the way you act outside school?

47 S: Well, I don't really do very much outside school, just—uh . . . I guess I don't really worry about it too much outside school.

48 C: Last time we talked you mentioned the possibility of going to summer school. Suppose you just dropped algebra completely, without making it up, not taking it now or anything . . .

49 S: Well, I'd feel kind of like quitting, and certainly wouldn't like to do that.

50 C: You feel as though once you've started you ought to finish.

51 S: Um-hmm.

52 C: Even if you fail.

53 S: Well, if I were failing, maybe it would be a better thing not to, but . . . I suppose it really would be a better thing to do, take math if I were failing.

54 C: You mean take another math course?

55 S: Yeah. Just take math instead.

56 C: How do you feel about this?

57 S: Well—uh—I'd rather take algebra. Of course, math is much easier. I'd probably have more time to do other things, but . . .

58 C: It'd be kind of hard to have to admit you couldn't handle it.

59 S: Yes. That's it really.

60 C: Would it hurt you more that other people then would know you weren't handling it or that for your own self-satisfaction?

61 S:   Probably for my own . . . what do you mean?

62 C:   Well, would you feel badly from your own point of view, just that you knew you weren't handling it, or would you be disturbed more by the fact that other people knew you weren't handling it?

63 S:   I guess I'd feel badly just if I knew I weren't handling it.

64 C:   Uh-huh.

65 C:   Just a matter of your own pride.

66 S:   Uh-huh. Of course it would be a little upsetting to have all, everybody else know you couldn't do it.

67 C:   If you managed to stick it through, though, and say, came out with a D, how would you feel about this?

68 S:   Well it'd be a little better than flunking. It wouldn't be as good as getting a better grade in another course.

69 C:   What you'd really like to do, of course, is stay in algebra and get a C or a B.

70 S:   Um-hmm. Or an A if possible.

71 C:   Yeah. Well, what seems to you now to be the most likely thing that will happen?

72 S:   Well, exactly what do you mean?

73 C:   Well, right now, if you were trying to predict what the situation will be in June, what your grade will be in algebra, what's the most likely thing that will happen?

74 S:   I'll probably get an awful grade. Take it over again or something. In summer school.

75 C:   If you get a D will you go to summer school then?

76 S:   Um-hmm.

77 C:   This isn't exactly the most desirable thing, I guess.

78 S:   No.

79 C:   Well, suppose you went to summer school, and got a C or passed anyway, got a C or better, then would you have another year of algebra coming up?

80 S:   I'd take algebra II, I guess. Go on.

81 C:   So really your problem now is just how to stay out of summer school, huh?

82 S:   I suppose so.

83 C:   Other than—well—other than the fact that you're kind of unhappy about the grades you're getting.
        (*Pause—3 minutes.*)

84 C:   There just doesn't seem to be much more to be said.

85 S:   Hmm. I don't know.
        (*Pause—2 minutes.*)

86 C:   Could you tell me any more about the way your mother feels about this?

87 S:   Well, she feels I should be doing better. Can't really think of anything else cuz I've really never stopped to think about it.

88 C:   Are there other members of your family?

89 S:   I live with my mother, grandmother, and grandfather.

90 C:   Do you talk about it at all with your mother and grandparents?

91  S:   Mother's been helping me with my algebra. It's still awfully hard.
92  C:   Once you've stated the problem, it's kind of hard to find what to do next.
93  S:   Yeah. (*Sigh.*) I never did really see what I would use the algebra for.
94  C:   It seems in a sense not a very useful subject.
95  S:   Yeah. I like to do sales work whenever I want and—uh—we took a test in social studies class, and I rated highest in persuasive work, trying to sell something, and . . .
96  C:   So really algebra doesn't have too much meaning for what you'll do later.
97  S:   No.
98  C:   Yet you feel as though you ought to take it. (*Pause.*) Especially in those areas where you do do well, like sales work, algebra doesn't seem to fit too well.
99  S:   Um-hmm.
100  C:  Does the problem then come down to trying to find your way out of this situation without getting your pride chopped down too much?
101  S:  Well, kind of.
(*Pause.*)
102  C:  Well, shall we call it a day for now and talk about it again next week?

In the second interview the counselor attempted to explore additional problem areas with the student. That is, he attempted to discover additional assertions that the student was making about himself. Statements 36, 38, 40, and 42 illustrate his initial attempt. He met with little success, but because he felt that there were important assertions and conflicts which hadn't been brought out, he tried a slightly different approach (44, 46) with a little more success (49–67).

The counselor's feeling that many assertions were either not being stated or not recognized by the student was reinforced by the section just referred to. Thus, from statement 84 through 91 he made a further attempt to help the student verbalize his difficulties. As a postscript, it may be of interest to know that in the third interview the counselor asked the student to complete a paper-and-pencil problem inventory, and then used the results as a method for bringing up problems for discussion. The student continued to have difficulty verbalizing assertions, but was willing and somewhat more able to discuss areas which he had checked on the inventory.

## PARTS AND OBJECTIVES

In a broad sense, a counseling session is begun, maintained, and terminated. One could, then, discuss counseling interviews in terms of these three parts. Obviously, this division is not an absolute one. Actual counseling interviews cannot be expected to conform to it. The division has value only as a convenience in talking about counseling, and not in planning actual counseling. To this end, then, we will discuss beginning an interview and the functions of the main body of an interview in the remainder of this chapter. Because the main function of beginning an interview is to facilitate what happens during the rest of the counseling session, the two "parts" are treated differently in the following discussions.

## Beginning a Counseling Interview

How do you begin a counseling interview? Sometimes you (the counselor) do not have to begin it; often you do, but in different ways with different students. Take, for example, the case of a ninth-grade student who is experiencing professional counseling for the first time. The student is asked to come to the counseling office during his free period. Here is how three different counselors might begin the interview.

COUNSELOR A

1 C:   Good morning, Hank. Won't you have a seat?

2 S:   Thank you.

3 C:   Well, I suppose you are pretty confused by being in high school and all, aren't you? Most students are, but you get used to it and pretty soon things seem much better. How do you like your teachers? Do we work you too hard here? (*Laughs.*)

4 S:   Yes, well I guess so. It's different from junior high.

5 C:   We met for just a few minutes during the first week of school and I told you then that I would meet with you several times while you were in high school. Well, today is our first counseling interview and it's for choosing your courses for the next three years.

6 S:   You mean I have to choose all my courses now? What do you mean?

7 C:   That's right, Hank. We think it works out better when students have a course plan for high school. We make the plan now so that you can get off to a good start. You see, we actually write your choices down on this form. Of course, if you have trouble, such as failing a course or something, it's possible to change your choices.

8 S:   Oh.

9 C:   Well, let's start by finding out what occupation you want to enter. What do you want to be?

10 S:   Gee, it's hard to say. I like math and science, so I thought maybe being a doctor might be good, or an atomic scientist, but they take so long.

11 C:   Well, if you want to be a scientist or doctor, you'll have to take a heavy college prep program. Probably college prep program A would be

best for you. You have several choices in that program. Here is a list of possible electives for next year. Which two appeal to you the most?

12 S:   Program A? What's that?

13 C:   It's a program. You know. We have different programs for students planning to do different things. Now, how about algebra and biology for next year? Then in your junior year you could take . . .

## COUNSELOR B

1 C:   Come in, Hank. Have a seat.

2 S:   Thanks.

3 C:   How have you been since our brief meeting the first week of school?

4 S:   Okay.

5 C:   That's good. How do you like high school now that you've been here a while?

6 S:   Pretty good. It was a little mixed up at first because everything was so new, but I got used to things.

7 C:   How are things going in class?

8 S:   Okay, I guess. It's hard to tell since we don't get grades on our daily work. My report cards weren't as good as they could have been, but I'm doing better this semester. At least I hope I am. That English is sure a lot of work, but I'm doing better.

9 C:   Well, that's good. Tell me, have you thought about your program for the next three years?

10 S:   What do you mean?

11 C:   I mean, have you thought about the courses you would like to take in high school?

12 S:   Sort of, but not very much.

13 C:   That's why I called you in today. During this time of the year all ninth-graders meet with their counselors to decide what courses they plan to take for the next three years. We plan this thing out so that you won't find yourself a senior wanting to take a certain course and not being able to because you didn't take the right courses during your sophomore and junior years.

14 S:   Gee, I don't know what I want to take when I'm a senior. That's a long way off.

15 C:   Not really, only three years. It's important for you to plan ahead. Maybe it would help if you were to tell me what you want to do when you finish school.

16 S:   Gee, I don't know.

17 C:   Well, do you want to go to college, or go to work, or join the service, or what?

18 S:   I don't know. I suppose I'll have to join the service sometime.

19 C:   In what branch are you interested?

## COUNSELOR C

1 C:   Come in, Hank, and have a chair.

2 S:   Thanks.

3 C:  I'm Mr. Jones. Do you remember our short visit at the beginning of the school year?

4 S:  Yeah.

5 C:  You may remember my saying that from time to time I would give you an opportunity to discuss your educational and vocational plans, or any problems that you might want to talk about. Do you?

6 S:  Yes. You said that you would be calling me in sometime in the second semester. I guess that's why I'm here.

7 C:  Yes, I thought you might want to talk about your high school program with me. Maybe discuss your plans for an occupation and what courses you want to take during the next three years. Would you like to do that?

8 S:  Yes, that's okay.

9 C:  Maybe it would help if I told you what you can expect from me. As I told you before, I'm your school counselor. Each counselor has a number of students with whom he counsels during their high school career. Students are assigned to counselors, but if at any time you want to see another counselor you are perfectly free to do so, even though I'm your regular counselor. You can change that, too, Hank. If at any time you would rather have another counselor for your regular counselor, let me know and I can arrange it for you. Okay?

10 S:  Yes, I see.

11 C:  Let me tell you a little about counseling. If you are like most students you have problems from time to time that you want to solve. High school students are faced with many decisions, and oftentimes these are difficult decisions to make. For example, you have to decide on courses, on what you want to do after high school, and on what extracurricular activities to join. Some students have personal and family problems about which they want to make decisions. What we do in counseling is to provide you with help in making these decisions. We can help you better understand your abilities and aptitudes, your interests, and so on. We can also help you get information about jobs and colleges. And, perhaps most important of all, we can discuss these things with you. Talking about these things often helps people to better understand themselves, and thus they can make better decisions throughout the rest of their lives. Maybe I've gone too fast. Can you tell me, now, what counseling is?

12 S:  I think I understand. You help kids choose courses and sometimes work out personal problems.

13 C:  You see counseling as a way to choose your courses.

14 S:  Well, I guess you help us with more things than that, like deciding what we are going to do for a vocation, I mean.

15 C:  Yes, that's what we try to do. Does that appeal to you?

16 S:  What do you mean?

17 C:  Do you want to discuss these things with me?

18 S:  Yes, that would probably help.

19 C:  Okay. There are a couple of other things which I want to tell you about counseling. First, you make all the decisions. I try to help you in the

ways I have described, but only you can make your own decisions. You may want to discuss the things we talk about during counseling with your parents or teachers, and that's certainly okay. But because you are the one that has to live by your decisions, it would be poor business for me to make them for you, even if I could, which I can't. The other thing is that whatever we say is confidential. That is, whatever we say is just between us. I don't discuss what we talk about with the principal, your teachers, your parents, or anyone else. Now, what does all this mean to you?

20 S:   Well, I think it means that you are not going to tell me what to do, and that you won't tell anyone what I say.

21 C:   Yes. Do you have any questions?

22 S:   No.

23 C:   Well, if you should think of some, please ask them.

24 S:   Okay.

25 C:   Now, one thing we like to have ninth-grade students do is to think through the next three years and the courses that they would like to take. We hope that in this way school can be of greater service to you by help-ing you prepare for your future. Maybe this is a good place to begin. Would you like to tell me what you hope to do in the future?

26 S:   I plan to go to college, of course. I'm not sure what I want to be, but it will probably be something like an architect or engineer.

27 C:   I see.

28 S:   I like math and I like to draw. I've already drawn some building plans—one for a gas station and one for an airport. My brother is studying to be an architect and he had to design an airport. He showed me some of his stuff and so I thought I would try it myself. He let me use some of his tools, you know, rulers and things. I never realized how much there was to drawing plans. I finished mine in a day and then when he told me all of the things that I hadn't done—boy! But anyway, my brother likes architecture and he thinks it would be good for me, too.

29 C:   You would like to do the same kind of work that your brother does.

These three interview excerpts portray counseling behavior dur-ing the first part of a counseling interview. They have been presented here to illustrate several aspects of the counseling process.

Unless there is good reason to believe that a student knows what to expect from counseling, it is important that a general explanation be offered to him during the first counseling session. This procedure is often referred to as *structuring*. Structuring is important for at least two reasons. First, it lets the student know what he can expect from the counselor, and what he should not expect. It helps to define the counselor's role. Often a counselor can also define the student's role in counseling, again in general terms. Second, structuring is important because it gives the student some idea of the counseling process. In supervising practicum-counselors the author has frequently found that two or three counseling sessions have taken place before the counselee discovered what was going on. Such uncertainty of purpose on the part of counselees inhibits the establishment of an effective counseling relationship.

Of the three interviewers, only Counselor C did a thorough job of structuring. Counselor A did little if any structuring. He dictated the purpose of the interview to the student in a few words and let it go at that. He failed to recognize or deal with the confusion and reticence evidenced by the student (6 S, 12 S), and he did not make any attempt to determine whether or not the student was even interested in discussing his program.

Counselor B did a partial job of structuring. He explained the purpose of the meeting, but failed to give the student an idea of how that was to be accomplished. Both Counselors A and B failed to discuss the responsibilities of the counselor and the counselee in the counseling process. We should not be surprised if these students failed to see any difference between counseling and advising.

Counselor C was careful to explain to the student both the purpose of the counseling sessions and the general nature of counseling. Notice that he was careful to appraise how well the student understood what had been said by getting some feedback (12 S, 13 C, 14 S, 15 C). The counselor also began to practice what he preached. After telling the student that he, the student, should make the decisions in counseling, the counselor asked him to decide whether or not he wanted to go on with the session.

Structuring is more than telling the counselee what to expect. It also involves behaving in a manner which will communicate the nature of the counseling relationship to the counselee. As a matter of fact, some counselors feel that verbal structuring as such is unnecessary, and that it actually misleads the client because, by itself, it is always inadequate. The latter point is valid, but it does not follow that structuring as such is misleading. Some counselors can establish the nature of counseling with some counselees in a brief period of time without ever engaging in formal structuring. Some students need more structuring than others, and a poor job of structuring can raise more anxiety than it alleviates. However, the high school counselor, because of his short-term contacts with students who are often unfamiliar with the counseling relationship, gains by structuring. It is important, of course, that he behave within the structure he has provided. If he does not, then structuring is of no positive value.

In order to counsel effectively, the counselor obviously needs to have good rapport with the counselee. Rapport is dynamic, and often varies within a single counseling session. For this reason, the counselor continually attempts to develop and maintain good rapport. Counselor A made little attempt to establish rapport with the student. Counseling has much in common with other person-to-person relationships. It is simply a matter of common sense to make the counselee feel at ease. Counselor B attempted to do this in terms of general small talk about school. Contrast the comments of Counselors A and B with those of Counselor C. Counselor C related the present session to a former meeting. He avoided small talk about any particular area of concern because he did not know what areas might be problem areas for the student. For example, Counselor B attempted to establish rapport by asking the student how he liked high school. This appears to be an innocent question, but if the student had been unhappy in high school and had developed very negative feelings about it, the question might have been quite disturbing to him. He might have reacted in several ways. He could have been frank about his feelings, but would probably have expected this to antagonize the counselor, who as far as the student perceived him was no different from other faculty members. Or, he might not have revealed his feelings, for fear of offending the counselor, and thus have begun counseling by holding back feelings. Neither reaction contributes to good rapport.

This is not to say that small talk at the beginning of an interview is inappropriate. Many interviews begin with some discussion about the weather, baseball, current events, or the like. The point is that the counselor should be keenly aware that whatever he says to the counselee is, in some way, going to influence initial rapport. When a school counselor says, "Hello, Jane, I don't know you but I know your older sister very well," he may be making a good beginning. It is also possible, depending on Jane's relations with her older sister, that he is destroying all chances for establishing rapport. The more a counselor knows about a counselee, the better he can predict the influence of his own behavior on the counselee.

The three interview excerpts also illustrate how acceptance can be used to help establish rapport. If counseling does nothing else, it should provide an atmosphere of acceptance in which the counselee can work through his problems without pressures and without the tensions of disconfirmations of his daily environment. The counselor gives neither his approval nor disapproval to the expressions of the counselee. He simply accepts. Obviously, in more subtle ways, acceptance can and does serve to reinforce the counselee. But it reinforces the student's self-confidence, his willingness to think about problems and make decisions, rather than the content of particular statements that he makes or feelings that he expresses. More will be said about the nature of acceptance in the following chapter. Notice, however, statements 14 S and 15 C of Counselor B. In a sense, the counselor was saying, "Let's plan for the future," and the student was asserting that the future was too far off to get very concerned about at that time. Counselor B reacted to this assertion by rejecting it and providing a rational argument for his rejection. Whether or not the counselor was correct is not the point. The counselor failed to accept the feeling expressed by the student. As a matter of fact, he even failed to recognize the feeling. It makes little sense to proceed with planning for the future unless the student feels that such planning is important. The result of the counselor's failure to deal with the student's assertion of feeling is evidenced in statements 16 S and 18 S. Rapport broke down and the student was reluctant to put himself in a position where the counselor could disconfirm more assertions.

It is difficult for the counselor to provide an accepting climate without knowing how well he and the counselee understand each other. For example, Counselor C was continually attempting to get feedback from the student so that he could appraise the student's understanding of his remarks. Notice that in statement 13 C he also fed back to the student his understanding of the student's remark. Statement 12 S indicates a certain misunderstanding on the part of the counselee. By reflecting this to the student, the counselor was able to test the misunderstanding by accepting what the student said. The counselor could have merely corrected the student, but this in itself would have been a rejection. That is, in effect the counselor would have been saying, "No, already you don't understand!"

Another point about beginning an interview is illustrated in the three examples. After some attention to structuring and rapport, it is important, of course, that the initial problem to be discussed should be stated. In the kind of interview illustrated, the initial outcome of the interview (making educational plans) and the actual problems to be discussed may be quite different. The counselor really has few ways of determining before the interview what, if any, problems need to be worked through as part of educational planning. One purpose of the beginning stage of a counselor-scheduled interview, then, is to identify problems which may influence educational planning (or whatever the stated purpose of the interview is). Notice that Counselor A, in statements 10 S and 11 C, ignored the student's concern over the preparation time involved in his tentative occupational choices. The student should have been given an opportunity to explore this consideration. To Counselor B, the student revealed a problem area that might influence his educational planning (statement 8 S). The student started several ideas in 8 S, but the counselor reacted to the final idea with "Well, that's good," thus apparently making the assumption that the matter of school marks no longer worried the student. In view of what the student said, the assumption is not necessarily valid. In contrast, notice the last several statements in the interview with Counselor C. The counselor was able to perceive and react to the student's assertion that he would like to be like his brother. The statement may or may not have been true, but it was important for the counselor to know of this attitude because of its potential influence on the student's vocational planning.

In this section, three aspects of beginning a counseling interview have been discussed—namely, structuring, establishing initial rapport through acceptance, and helping the counselee state his problems. It should be evident that as suggested earlier these aspects overlap considerably. The counselor does not structure, then establish rapport, and then help the client state his problem. At the start of the interview, he attempts to make a beginning on all three. As counseling progresses, restructuring, rebuilding rapport and redefining the problem may all become necessary. Nevertheless, specific attention to these considerations from the beginning will result in more effective counseling.

## Objectives of the Counseling Interview

The previous section described and illustrated the beginning part of a counseling interview with secondary school students. No formula was presented because none is available that would be universally applicable. The considerations discussed, however, are relevant to nearly all counseling interviews. Now let us focus on the purposes and functions of the main part of the counseling interview. This is an even more difficult task. The similarity of one high school counseling interview to another, evident at the beginning of counseling, diminishes considerably once the interview begins. Because each counselee and each counselor are different, the counseling relationship they develop is unique. However, an orderly view of counseling may be had if we look at it from several general perspectives: first, its general purpose or function; second, counseling technique; and, third, the several kinds of interview tasks and the procedures employed to accomplish these. As indicated earlier in this chapter, technique and procedure will be discussed in the following two chapters. The remainder of this chapter will deal with the main body of the interview in terms of the general functions of counseling.

One major purpose of counseling is to help the student understand himself and his environment, such understanding being requisite for making meaningful and effective decisions. This purpose can be accomplished to a great extent by noncounseling activities. Group instruction and discussion can often be employed effectively. There is a point, however, one that is probably different for each student, after which he can benefit most in self-understanding from counseling. For example, well-planned group instruction on test results can be beneficial to most students. Students can be taught the language of test results and given descriptions of their test performances. Then they can listen to lectures and carry out exercises to insure a thorough understanding. This essentially is the method of teaching, and an effective one in most cases. For example, the history of World War II can be made to come alive for most students through effective teaching methods. Through such experience, few students will achieve a specifically accurate notion of the events and their causes. Rather, they will gain a general understanding which, for most, is sufficient. Few students, through teaching, will come to understand what the content they have studied means to them personally. This, too, is not crucial. However, when the student is attempting to understand his own scholastic aptitude, for instance, as a basis for making decisions that he will have to live with for the rest of his life, it is extremely important that he understand to his greatest ability just what the test results mean to him. Providing such understanding usually involves something more than traditional instruction. It entails helping the student relate the test results to the normative data the counselor has, and to his own unique experiences and assertions about himself. This is a task that is probably new to him, a task he may find confusing and often threatening. It may disconfirm many of his assertions, raise new problems, and stimulate conflicts. It is with these aspects of student problems and behavior that counseling is intended to help. A function of counseling is to help the student accomplish current self-understanding so as to provide a meaningful basis for future self-understanding. The factors involved in self-understanding include abilities, achievements, aptitudes, interest, values, and relations with others. These will be treated specifically in Chapter 6.

In understanding various aspects of their environment, as in understanding themselves, students can get a great deal of information through regular teaching methods. But, in order to understand what this information means to them, students need opportunities to relate it to their own experiences and perceptions. They need to understand what high school can mean to them, the personal implications of non-occupational job entailments, the influences of family and friends on their educational and vocational plans, and other matters of like importance. Counseling can help students accomplish such tasks.

Another general function of counseling is to help the student accept information about himself and his environment—not accept in the sense of finality or predeterminism, but in the sense of behaving according to his self-understanding. The difference between understanding and acceptance is not always clear. Indeed, some counselors feel that real understanding implies accepting in the sense just given. An example or two will point up, however, the distinction between understanding and accepting.

A senior in high school had seen the results of several achievement-test batteries he had taken during the last few years. He had discussed these in a social studies class and had talked with his counselor about whether or not the achievement scores indicated he could be successful in college. The scores were such that his chances for remaining in college were about 10 out of 100. The counselor had worked through these data with the boy, as well as other data pertinent to his decision. The counselor felt that the student understood his chance for success in college and on several occasions he had obtained feedback to this effect. However, as a senior the boy applied to several colleges and entered competition for several scholarships. He was not accepted at any of the colleges, and the counselor received reports of his low scores on the scholarship examinations. He saw the student again and was reassured that the student understood his scholastic aptitude and achievement status. The point is, of course, that while the student understood his status, he had not accepted it. He did not behave in terms of what he understood about himself.

Another student, a junior girl, disclosed to her counselor the fear that she was pregnant. With the counselor's assistance, the girl informed her parents. The counselor helped to arrange a medical examination which confirmed the pregnancy. The counselor then spent several sessions with the girl and her parents, both individually and together, helping them understand the implications of the problem as it affected the girl's remaining in school, and describing several means of referring the student to appropriate agencies for help. Both the parents and the girl gave every indication of understanding the implications and the steps involved in a referral. However, the girl remained in school. On a follow-up the counselor discovered that the parents had made no attempt to complete the referral he had helped them initiate. He saw both the girl and her parents again, learned that they thoroughly understood the whole situation but had simply not been able to accept it.

These two illustrations are dramatic, but they are atypical only in degree. Counselors continually meet with students who to a lesser degree have not accepted what they understand about themselves. They have begun to experience disconfirmation of their assertions and they show redundant behavior. No amount of understanding alone can provide them with a basis for making more appropriate decisions. They must accept as well as understand.

As we have seen in Chapter 2, counseling sessions with secondary school students are frequently concerned with helping students defined decisions that need to be made. More is involved here than helping students *identify* problems. Most students are aware of their problems to some degree. For example, an underachieving student, while not able to analyze his difficulty, can usually recognizes that it exists, and he typically experiences concern over it. Similarly, students who are unable to establish satisfactory peer relationships are of course troubled and recognize an unsatisfactory state of affairs, even though they have not been able to see the causes of their predicament. Counselors can serve students by helping them *clarify* problems.

One method of accomplishing this is to help students discover the various alternative courses of action available to them, and the probable incidental effects of each. In terms of our basic frame of reference, the student is faced with the responsibility of making general or specific decisions, or both. The counselor can help him to perceive the various alternatives (including the decision not to make decisions). A more logical approach might suggest that the counselor make a somewhat didactic analysis of a problem situation before helping the counselee clarify needed decisions. Such analysis is unnecessary, however, when attention is focused on decisions. In the process of clarifying alternatives and defining decisions, the student will attend to the pertinent factors in his problem, and will become less apt to confuse basic issues with side issues regarding the cause of his present situation. If causal past events are important to needed decisions, they will be considered. If they are not important, they will be given little, if any, attention. A basic function of the counselor, from this point of view is to help the student maintain the decision-making frame of reference. The following case summary is an illustration.

At the beginning of his senior year, Bill saw his counselor for a scheduled senior interview. He had planned to attend college ever since enrolling in high school and had taken the college preparatory program, maintaining a strong C average for two years. During his junior year, Bill's counselor had discussed aptitude and achievement test scores with him. Every standardized measure of scholastic aptitude available for Bill placed him below the 55 percentile. Standardized measures of achievement were appropriate to his aptitude scores. In the interview, the counselor raised the question of college attendance.

C:  Bill, would you like to tell me about how your college plans are coming along?
S:  I still plan to go State U if I can get in.
C:  You're a little concerned about being admitted to State U?
S:  A little. I think my grades could be better. I mean—they're average. I haven't any F's or D's, but they could be higher. My G.P.A., I mean.
C:  You have just a little over a C average, right?
S:  Yes, and from what people say, it should be at least a B. I can apply though, at least. That's the only way to find out, isn't it? Do you think they will let me in? What if I can bring my grades up this year? If I could get all B's this year, that would help, wouldn't it?
C:  That would raise your total G.P.A., wouldn't it? What would be involved in accomplishing this, Bill?
S:  Harder work, I guess. And really sticking to my decision to do it. It

would take a lot of work, especially since my senior courses will be tougher than any I've had before.

C: Making up your mind to work harder and staying with it?

S: If I can do it, yes.

C: If you can make up your mind?

S: No, if I can work harder. I mean, if I work hard, have I the ability?

C: We talked about ability last year. Do you remember some of the things we discussed?

S: Yes, very well. I'm a little above average, and we thought that I would have to work very hard to succeed at State U. I've been trying to apply myself since our talk.

C: You're taking the science and math courses required as prerequisites for pharmacy majors, too.

S: I almost got a D in chemistry.

C: Bill, when did you first begin to think about being a pharmacist?

S: In junior high school, I guess. A neighbor was a pharmacist and talked to me about it. After that I've just sort of assumed that I would go into pharmacy.

C: It just sort of happened?

S: Yes.

C: Would you like to take a few minutes and think about your decision to become a pharmacist? I'm not trying to change your mind, Bill. However, deciding to go to college is obviously one of the most important decisions that a person makes. It may help to talk about it. Do you want to?

S: Okay. Where do we start?

C: Well, perhaps we could get the total picture by seeing just how many alternatives you have open to you when you finish high school. What are some of them?

S: You mean things I could do?

C: Yes, for example, you could decide to go to State U. What are some other possible decisions?

S: I see—I could go to work, or join the services, or just bum around— that's a possibility. Or I could—well—regarding a school—enroll in a trade school, or become an apprentice. We read about those things in a vocations unit last year. Or locally, I could go to City Junior College—or as I said, State U.

C: There seem to be many alternatives.

S: I could think of more.

C: You didn't mention any 4-year college other than State U. Is that a possible alternative?

S: Sure.

C: Would you like to tell me how you feel about some of these? For example, why are they, or aren't they, appealing to you?

S: Well, work, for example. I mean right after high school, doesn't offer much future. I think that an education should come first. You almost have to have an education these days to get any place.

C: An education is important in itself.

S: In a way—but really it's what you can do with what you learn.
C: Perhaps it's not so much the way you obtain vocational abilities, but having them that counts.
S: Yes, but college is the only way to learn some occupations.
C: How do you feel about occupations which involve training, but not necessarily college training?
S: I don't know much about them, but I wouldn't have any objections as long as they had a future.
C: You want the security of vocational training. It's not just the present but the future that is important.
S: That's why college seems so important—for the future.
C: Is it college or having some occupational abilities to build on?
S: The abilities. I guess the rest is up to a person himself.
C: If you are correct, then what things do you know about yourself that should be a part of your decision to go to State U?
S: I see what you mean. We're back to my ability again. Even if I get in— there's a good chance I would flunk out. You know, I've worried about that before, quite a bit. But I just can't see going to work after graduation.
C: You want more education.
S: What you had me list a few minutes ago—can you tell me about other ways to get training?—with a future, I mean? Like, for example, what about J.C.'s? Are they all like the one we have?

In the case just cited, the counselor tried to help the student approach his problem from the decision-making perspective. Obviously, the student's problem had many complexities which were not mentioned. One of these, the factor of status and peer group values, eventually was introduced in the counseling session by the counselor. Other factors were not, even though they were important from a causal perspective; the point being that a causal perspective was irrelevant. The student's problem was one of making an appropriate educational decision and doing so with awareness of possible entailments. Such a goal is accomplished if the counselee is helped to interfere with his on-going behavior, and thus allowed to replace it with more appropriate behavior.

Two additional counseling functions that occur quite frequently are also illustrated in the interview. The first is motivating the student to work on a problem. Bill, for example, would probably have gone along with his plans until some crisis forced the issue. Had he applied to the State University for admission, and been turned down, he would have been forced into a new pattern of behavior. Had he been accepted and failed, or accepted as a freshman and rejected by the pharmacy department, he would have again been forced into a crisis situation. True, he might have been able to fulfill his educational plan, but there was considerable evidence to the contrary. In either case, chance seemed to be the basic determinant until the counselor helped motivate Bill to work on his problem and, thus, at least anticipate what would most probably happen were he to maintain his decision.

The case of Bill also illustrates how students may be helped to distinguish between immediate and ultimate implications of decisions. This is one important area of growth during adolescence in our culture. In counseling sessions there is frequent opportunity, and in fact, necessity, for helping students make such distinctions. In the latter part of the interview, Bill and the counselor worked through the status implications of college attendance. Such things as the persistency of peer status, the influence of college failure on status, and the changes in status symbols during a person's lifetime were discussed. Bill gave indications that he had been thinking only in terms of the immediate implications of his decision, to the neglect of ultimate implications.

There is one further basic function of counseling. Regardless of the particular problem content of a particular counseling session, counselors should be concerned with making it easier for a student to benefit from future counseling and other assistance. Certainly, one or two counseling sessions will not prepare a student to solve all of life's problems. While a counselor hopes that his help will not be limited to immediate problems, but will carry over to problems and decisions in the future, it is obvious that other assistance will be available to counselees during the coming years. A do-or-die, do-it-all-now attitude can have an undesirable influence on a counselor's effectiveness with students. It sets unrealistic and unreasonable criteria for counseling, and thus dooms counselors to feelings of unnecessary frustration and failure. By helping the counselee perceive his problems in a broad perspective of long-range implications, and by doing so through a counselee-counselor relationship which emphasizes self-acceptance, honest decisions, and self-responsibility, the counselor helps the counselee to derive greater benefit from future assistance. As a student, and as an adult, the counselee will receive from others counseling, advice, enticement, threats, arguments—all of which may be useful to some extent, depending upon his ability to relate to others with awareness and acceptance of his own strengths and weaknesses. To reiterate, an effective counseling experience, in addition to helping with immediate problems and providing skills for future decisions, should also increase the ability of the individual to benefit from the noncounseling assistance offered by others.

### Suggested References

The following references discuss and illustrate the counseling interview from varying points of view.

Brayfield, Arthur H., "Interviewing," in *Modern Methods of Counseling*, Appleton-Century-Crofts, 1950, Part 5.

Callis, R., P. C. Polmantier, and E. C. Roeber, *A Casebook of Counseling*, Appleton-Century-Crofts, 1955.

Patterson, C. H., *Counseling and Psychotherapy; Theory & Practice*, Harper, 1959.

Porter, E. H., Jr., *An Introduction to Therapeutic Counseling*, Houghton Mifflin, 1950.

Rogers, Carl R., "The Case History of Herbert Bryan," in *Counseling and Psychotherapy*, Houghton Mifflin, 1942, Part IV.

Snyder, W. U. (ed.), *Casebook of Non-Directive Counseling*, Houghton Mifflin, 1947.

Tyler, Leona E., "The Counseling Interview" and "The Decision-Making Interview," in *The Work of the Counselor*, Appleton-Century-Crofts, 1953, chaps. II, IX.

# CHAPTER 5

# Counseling Techniques

Techniques in counseling are not like techniques in surgery or law. The counselor has nothing analogous to surgical skills or legal maneuvers with which he can accomplish his objectives. His main stock in trade is his ability to understand and communicate with counselees. To say that he accomplishes this by using various techniques is both correct and a little misleading. For example, a skilled counselor can read a counseling interview typescript, and judging according to predetermined categories of counseling techniques, can identify most of the counselor responses as one or another of these. In this sense, the concept of counseling techniques is a valid one. It becomes misleading when we assume that during the counseling interview the counselor deliberately chooses this technique or that technique by name or nature and uses it to accomplish a specific task. Certainly this is done to some extent by all counselors. There are probably some techniques which, more than others, counselors tend to employ purposefully. For the most part, however, the way the counselor responds depends on what he is attempting to communicate to the counselee.

Because of this, many writers have thought it unnecessary or unwise to give much emphasis to counseling techniques. They have assumed that concentration on techniques will lead to a superficial kind of counseling, and further, that techniques can be developed only through experience in counseling. The latter point is valid, but there are at least two considerations peculiar to secondary school counseling which justify devoting considerable attention to techniques per se.

In the first place, high school counselors in general undergo a different kind of professional preparation than do counselors in college and university counseling centers, medical institutions, and private practice. Counselors in these situations usually have a longer period of professional preparation than the typical high school counselor, and one that includes at least a year or more of interning. Thus they are in a position to develop counseling techniques in a more or less intuitive manner during relatively extensive interning. Although a number of secondary school counselors spend some time in a practicum or field experience course, their experience cannot realistically be considered comparable to an internship. Whether or not internship should be provided is not the point here. However, because the school counselor typically does not have an extensive opportunity to develop techniques through interning or its equivalent, it seems reasonable to provide him with some fairly specific instruction in techniques to compensate for the lack. Of course, the student must approach the section on techniques with the reservations which had been stated earlier.

The second justification for giving special attention to counseling techniques per se stems from the differences between the working environment of the high school counselor and that of other counselors. The high school counselor is much less clinically oriented. While he does have a few counselees who come to him or are referred to him with relatively severe problems (that is, problems which are seriously inhibiting daily behavior), most of his counseling is more developmental than remedial or preventive. He sees students on a fairly routine basis about fairly typical adolescent problems. He sees large numbers of students for relatively brief contacts. The counselor working in nonsecondary school situations, on the other hand, counsels primarily with individuals who have developed rather severe psychological problems. He typically sees fewer counselees than does the high school counselor, and his counseling contacts are of considerably greater length. Further, the primary and often single purpose of the organization for which he works is therapeutic. Helping students through counseling is only one purpose of the secondary school. In most schools counseling is perceived, to varying degrees, as something extra—a special service for getting a particular task accomplished. The primary purpose, and thus the basic orientation of the schools, is to educate people, not to help them get well.

Thus, the nonschool counselor works in an environment that is much more conducive to developing counseling competencies than that of the school counselor. His orientation, and that of many or all of his fellow workers, is counseling. His job is much more homogeneous than that of the school counselor, who spends much of his time in non-counseling guidance activities, and few, if any of his colleagues (depending upon the size of his school) are counselors. Thus he must lean heavily on his professional preparation as a basis for developing effective counseling techniques.

To sum up, counseling techniques as such are useful as descriptive categories rather than methods of procedure; they cannot be understood without practice and experimentation; but, because of the school counselor's unique situation, it is important that his preparation include a consideration of these techniques. With this rationale in mind, let us move on to consider some techniques of counseling.

Counseling techniques can be viewed from several perspectives. Perhaps the most useful one is that of a *continuum of lead*. The concept of leading in counseling refers to the extent to which the counselor takes responsibility for the content of the interview. This should not be confused with the ratio of counselor-counselee talk in an interview, although the two are necessarily related. A counselor using very leading techniques more or less determines the topics considered and contributes his own feelings about the client and his problem on a verbal level. At the other extreme, a counselor employing as few highly leading techniques as possible lets the counselee determine topics and what is said about the topics. He works, verbally at least, only with what the counselee contributes to the interview, and carefully avoids verbalizing his own feelings about what the counselee states. He attempts to help the counselee better understand himself and his environment within the bounds of content and feeling of the counselee's verbalizations.

Selected counseling techniques distributed over a hypothetical continuum of lead (not based on actual data) look somewhat as follows:

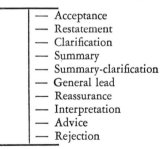

LEAST AMOUNT OF LEADING

— Acceptance
— Restatement
— Clarification
— Summary
— Summary-clarification
— General lead
— Reassurance
— Interpretation
— Advice
— Rejection

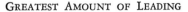

GREATEST AMOUNT OF LEADING

Information giving as a counseling technique is not placed on the continuum because the amount of leading it represents varies depending on how and when it is given. This point will be discussed later. Let us turn now to a discussion and illustration of each of the techniques.

## Acceptance

The technique of acceptance is employed by the counselor when he wishes to communicate to the student that what has been said is understood. It is the simplest means of communicating this to the counselee. It does not interrupt the counselee's talk, and, further, encourages him to continue. It usually takes the form of silence or a one- or two-word phrase, or simply a smile, nod of the head, or bodily gesture. .

S: So, after I failed the test I was really disappointed—you know, hardly knew what to do or say to my folks.

C: I see.

S: I didn't tell them for a while, but this was worse since I knew I would have to soon.

C: (*Nods his head.*)

S: Boy, was that a terrible wait—knowing each night that they might ask me about it. But oh gosh, what a spot!

C: Uh-huh.

In the illustration the counselor communicated to the student that he understood and accepted what was being said. He wanted to do this in such a way as not to interrupt the continuity of the student's remarks. The counselor was really trying to communicate something like this: "I understand what you are saying and how you feel about it. I am not making any value judgment about the behavior you describe or the way you feel about it. I simply accept it. Please continue." Most counselors are able to communicate this by simple acceptance techniques without becoming more verbally involved. The possible effects of responding more verbally, are (1) there is some danger in disturbing the continuity of what the counselee is saying, and (2) the counselor may become involved in the content of the student's story. The disadvantages of the first effect are obvious. The disadvantage of the second effect is the possibility of inhibiting the counselee's willingness to reveal his own feelings.

## Restatement

Restatement is employed for several reasons. First, it conveys acceptance to the client. Second, it often gives the client a brief rest and a chance to collect his thoughts before going on with his story. Third, it serves as a means of feedback to the counselee. That is, by simply repeating what the counselee has said, the counselor checks the accuracy of his own understanding, and at the same time gives the student an opportunity to hear what he has just said and to clarify his statement if it is not what he meant to say. Restatement, with use of voice inflection, can emphasize the feelings behind a counselee's remarks as well as their content.

S:   So I guess my biggest problem is to decide whether to take the financial risk of going away to college.

C:   You think your biggest problem is deciding whether to take the financial risk of going away to college?

S:   Yes. But I guess I could solve that all right by a taking a light load and getting a part-time job. But then it would take longer to finish school. Gee, what do you think I should do?

C:   You would like to have me decide which is the best alternative for you.

As is evident in the illustration, restatement adds no new content to the counseling session. It involves leading to the extent that the counselee is able to achieve new understanding through having the counselor repeat what he has just stated. Students often achieve significant understandings from the use of restatement, primarily because they often fail to perceive the implication of a statement until they hear it repeated by the counselor. This phenomenon is one common to many kinds of conversation. People in positions of authority, for example, often repeat what someone has just said to them. Other examples are parents repeating what their child has just declared in an angered state, a supervisor repeating the incorrect answer of a worker, or simpler yet, the many times we repeat to ourselves a thought which suddenly seems pregnant with implications.

## Clarification

Clarification entails definite leading and the counselor's contribution of something new to the content of the counseling session. It is typically used in response to a student's statement which the counselor feels is an important expression but expressed so poorly that a simple restatement would tend to perpetuate the ambiguity. In a sense the counselor may be saying, "You've got the facts, old boy, but not in the correct order."

S:   I'm not quite sure. She's [mother] got a lot of strange ideas on it. She seems to think I'm quite remarkable. I personally don't think I am. I think

I'm different, and I suppose people think I'm a bit of a genius; and I think that maybe I'm a bit of a genius or I'm totally insane, but geniuses aren't really that rare. People seem to think they are.

C: Uh-huh.

S: My mother seems to think I have trouble associating with my contemporaries. That is a bit of a problem because I don't consider them my contemporaries. I don't get a big blast out of smoking cigarettes and I don't like the taste of wine particularly. If they want to go out and wreck their lungs, not to mention their throats, that's their business. I don't think it's right. I think it's a waste.

C: You feel that your mother doesn't understand that associating with your contemporaries or age mates would involve compromising your own standards of appropriate behavior.

In terms of our basic frame of reference, the counselor uses clarification when he feels that he can better state an assertion made by the student, and in such a way that he will be close enough to the counselee's actual expression so as not to lose him. This latter consideration is a potential difficulty in using clarification. The counselor may misjudge the extent to which the counselee actually understands what he has expressed—that is, the fact may be that the counselee is not ready to understand or accept what he has expressed, rather than that he has not done a very effective job of verbalizing his feelings. In such a case, "clarification" can lead the student to believe that the counselor does not understand what has been said, which is partly true.

Other considerations make clarification a particularly difficult technique to develop. Assuming that the counselor really does understand what has just been expressed, it is not a simple task to select the phrases which will communicate this to the counselee. There is a difference in perceiving what the counselee has expressed and verbalizing this perception for him. An even greater difficulty is that of timing. If the counselor could somehow stop the interview for a few moments at just the right time, he could review to himself what has been expressed, select the most appropriate phrasing, and then start the interview again with a clarification. Unfortunately, nothing even remotely like this is possible. Counseling is so dynamic that frequently by the time the counselor has seen a need for clarification the counselee has changed the interview content so as to make the clarification inappropriate.

One of the best methods of developing clarification skill is for the counselor to listen to recordings of his own interviews and attempt to identify places where clarification would have been appropriate. Finding these, he should stop the recorder and attempt to verbalize the clarification, and then check its validity by replaying the expressions clarified. Systematic practice of this kind tends to develop the counselor's confidence and skill so that he can begin experimenting more with clarification in actual counseling sessions.

## Summary

Summary is a technique involving an even greater amount of leading. This may not seem logical at first, but consider for a moment what happens when one person summarizes what another has said. It is essentially abstracting. From a given segment of an interview, the counselor selects those ideas and feelings which seem most important and attempts to feed them back to the student in a more organized form. Obviously, the counselor's summary statement may be inaccurate or unacceptable to the student, thus destroying rapport. However, when summary is effective it transposes various counselee expressions into relatively clear assertive statements, providing the counselee with a firm base point, so to speak, from which to continue.

C: You feel that your family really want to do the right thing for you but they are not sure how to go about it?

S: Yes, I like them and don't want to offend them in any way, but I have my own life to live, too. They really don't know as much about this [appropriate school courses] as I do. They're a little outdated. I mean that's natural and all, and I'm sorry they are, but it's so.

C: You're sorry that they don't understand, but it's a fact that they don't.

In the illustration above the counselor summarized a relatively brief counselee expression. There are times when the counselor wishes to summarize a longer segment of an interview. While this can sometimes be accomplished with a simple summary statement, it is frequently more appropriate to use a technique which we can label *summary-clarification*. By definition, the larger the segment being summarized, and more abstract the summary. The more abstract the summary becomes, the greater the contribution of the counselor to the inverview content.

(The student has been discussing concern over petting with his girl friend.)

C: You felt that you became quite involved, but still always had control of the situation.

S:  In that I realized what I was doing. But afterward, the after-effects, the only thing, I feel bad sometimes because she feels bad and hurt, and how or why I don't understand. Well mainly, from what I can understand, this is the first time she has gotten this far involved with a person, and there is bound to be some little guilt feelings anyhow, you know. And with me, I'm more concerned about the intentions of both our actions, rather than the actions themselves. That's what I place this judgment on—whether I should get this involved with her. I like her a lot, personally, and I tell her I love her. I don't want to say that here, because that might not sound—I've never done anything to prove I've loved her. I mean, the reason that you want to self-sacrifice for a person—I'd do anything for her, and I could probably think of things to do for her and all this and that, but I don't want to come out and say that to you, because it might not be really true. But I tell it to her, because as far as I'm concerned in my relationship to her, it's true. I wouldn't want to say objectively, but perhaps subjectively I could call it love. But anyhow, I like her a lot, and she likes me a lot. So, therefore, the question that would enter into my mind is would both of our intentions be for love or for fun—that would be the important thing to me. And although fun is obviously a part of it, I think that is more with the actions than the intentions, although it primarily could be for fun, you know.

C:  Uh-huh.

S:  But I think as it involves me personally, the fun would be rather in the actions, if you want to call it fun, than the elements of like would be in the intentions. And, as far as she's concerned, actually she claims that it's a matter of love as intentions. But that's the way I feel—occasionally, she gets these feelings—after the first time she was sort of shook; last time she didn't get too shook. She said she was just a little worried, you know, and I tried to soothe her conscience, because she was somewhat conscious about it. I asked her if her intentions governed it, and asked her what it was. I don't have any after-effects unless I'm not sure of the intentions, you know. That would be the only time that I would have an after-effect—concern over her intentions.

C:  You feel then that it is probably desirable, if this kind of emotional relationship continues, that you both should be really sure about your final intentions. It also seems that you might feel that her intentions toward you are somewhat definite, but possibly there's some doubt in your mind as to how you feel about her. You're not quite sure whether or not it is something real deep, or something less than this, and this uncertainty worries you.

## General Lead

A general lead involves the counselor's *asking* the student to do something, and thus quite openly requires the counselor to take considerable responsibility for the interview content. General leads can be phrased in a number of ways, thus allowing some flexibility in the degree of responsibility the counselor assumes. A general lead which allows the counselee a great deal of freedom in what he talks about is a question such as, "Would you like to tell me something about yourself?" A general lead with less flexibility for the counselee is given in the following excerpt:

S: Yes, well I have no one that you would call a boy friend. Boys don't particularly like me.
C: Can you tell me a little more about that?

In this illustration the counselor wasn't sure just what he wanted, but felt that the area was important to explore. While the general lead is a response to a specific assertion made by the student, it is still sufficiently vague to place the responsibility for the content of the ensuing remarks with the counselee.

The following excerpt illustrates the use of a general lead by the counselor when his intent is to have the counselee discuss a particular topic. While the counselee is still asked to determine the content of the interview, the counselor is suggesting definite topical limits.

C: Well, last week you mentioned that there was something that you didn't like about yourself. Do you want to explain that a little more?
S: Well, there are things about myself which I just don't like. You know, a person has things which he instinctively dislikes. I used to have people say . . .

A second major kind of general lead is probing. The counselor sometimes feels it important that a counselee continue to discuss a particular point within a topic. The reason depends upon the situation and the counselor's orientation. The counselor may simply want to know more about the topic or the student's feelings about the topic. More likely, he may feel that by probing he can lead the student to a new perception. A probing lead might also be used in a situation where the counselor suspects that additional ramifications of a problem might be revealed in a further specific discussion of the topic. In any event, when the counselor uses a probing lead he is asking the student a direct question about a specific topic.

The strong possibility of eliciting hostility and rejection by probing the student in a threatening area should be obvious. Techniques for dealing with hostility toward the counselor will be considered in the following chapter. An example of probing follows:

S: Well, there are things about myself which I just don't like. A person has things which he instinctively dislikes. I used to have Sam bellow at me in loud and mighty tones. (*Talks about Sam, her director in an acting group.*) There are different reasons why you dislike a person; you dislike one of these pious quacks, or a person with a dictatorial attitude, or a person who is bigoted. Well, there are things about me I don't like. In the same instinctive way I just don't like them.

C:  Like what?

S:  Oh, I don't like some of my attitudes. I don't know how I'm ever going to change them. But I don't like them. I have attitudes about certain type people which I shouldn't have. Dad says they are just a precaution, but I don't think I should have them. (*Talks about characters at school that she calls greasies.*) I just instinctively dislike them. It has its problems because I'm also afraid of them. I don't like the attitudes I have. Like education. I don't think it's a safe attitude to have. It isn't practical. (*Talks about neighbors she doesn't like and talks about the fact that she's afraid of dogs because one almost put her eye out.*)

C:  Are you worried because there are so many different types of people you don't like?

## Reassurance

The technique of reassurance is actually used on two levels. Its position on the leading continuum is determined by the second level. In a sense the counselor is continually reassuring the counselee. He is saying to the student, "You are doing fine in your role as a counselee. You are supposed to be verbalizing your feelings. There is no need to feel threatened or guilty about telling me these things. This is exactly what we are here for." In this sense, the counselor is reassuring the student in respect to the counseling process. This kind of reassurance is an important aspect of maintaining rapport, but typically it is done implicitly and by inference. The technique of simple acceptance was discussed earlier. Reassurance at the second level goes beyond acceptance in that the counselor agrees with the counselee's statement or overtly supports his assertion. Inexperienced counselors frequently make inappropriate use of reassurance because of their tendency to become psychologically involved or engrossed in what the counselee is saying. Reassurance employed unintentionally, without a real purpose, can turn counseling into a conversation of the "gripe session" variety. Undoubtedly, whatever catharsis takes place can be helpful to the student, but so can a good hot bath!

There are three general reasons for using reassurance, in the second sense, during counseling. The first is that the counselor wants to give tentative support to a counselee as a means of building up the counselee's courage to discuss a particularly difficult situation. The counselor offers reassurance as a crutch for getting through a painful topic, but intends to remove it gradually as the counselee gains the ability to accept disconfirmations for what they are. The obvious hazards are that (1) reassurance once offered may be difficult to withdraw, and (2) a reassuring counselor (in the second sense) may appear to the student as just another adult who doesn't really understand, and the development of rapport may be inhibited.

The second reason for using reassurance is that there may seem to be no other means of getting a counselee to continue discussing a topic. The topic may not be especially painful to the student, but he may not see it as significant and may not want to discuss it. The counselor, however, may suspect that a discussion of the topic will be beneficial to the student. When other less leading techniques fail, the counselor, by using reassurance, implies that the topic is important. The counselee, seeing the status given to the topic by the counselor, may then become interested in pursuing the topic further.

Finally, reassurance can be employed as a very direct way of confirming an assertion. Again, however, this involves the disadvantage of solving the student's problem for him, instead of helping him to solve his own problems. Illustrations of each of the above three uses of reassurance follow.

(1)

(The student has mentioned her feelings towards her recently divorced parents, but has not been able to discuss these feelings.)

C:  You feel that your parents did not consider your well-being?
S:  Yes. (*Pause.*)
C:  Would you like to tell me a little more about that?
S:  Well, I don't know how important it is to deciding on a college. It obviously hurt me, but I simply accepted it, that's all.
C:  It wasn't very fair to you, was it?
S:  No, but I can't let it mess up my whole life.
C:  Then, it is important, isn't it? Worrying about it may have an important influence on your college plans, and thus your whole life.
S:  I know. If only it hadn't happened this way. It just takes all the interest out of school and college. I worry, and then worry over worrying . . .

(2)

S:  The only trouble with not taking English A [college prep course] is that if I do decide to go to college, I would be deficient in English requirements. I can worry about that bridge when I come to it, if I do, though.

C: You don't want to take English A unless you know for sure that you will need it for college.

S: Yes. It just isn't interesting to me and unless I knew I had to have it, it would be miserable.

C: Students sometimes feel that way about some courses, and it's certainly understandable. At the same time, deficiencies can really restrict you if you should want to go to college. Do you think it would be worth taking a few minutes to see just what effect this particular deficiency might have if you should decide to go to college?

S: Well, yes, what would it do to me?

(3)

S: I think I have the ability to do a good job as class president, if I won, that is. But my Dad says that even if I were elected the kids wouldn't do what I wanted. He says that the hoity-toy run things, and that I'm just asking for trouble. He said I could do what I want, but that I was sure kidding myself.

C: Because your family is not as well off as some, your father thinks you wouldn't be respected as class president? But you think that you would?

S: Yes. I never have trouble. It may sound conceited, but I don't think they would have asked me to run if they didn't respect me some at least. But I don't know, maybe he's right.

C: You certainly have had their respect before, haven't you? Your other elected offices and your activity record show that.

## Interpretation

Interpretation, in the traditional sense, is a technique employed frequently by counselors with a depth or Freudian orientation. There are numerous complicated constructs and assumptions which make up the rationale for interpretation. It is neither appropriate nor possible to present these here. The very general statement will suffice that, among other things, interpretation involves explaining to the counselee what his behavior (in the broadest sense) really means. Perhaps the most commonly cited illustration of interpretation is in regard to dreams. Depth-oriented counselors sometimes interpret the significance of dreams to their counselees. Also, it is common for counselors to interpret the significance of other behavior to counselees. For example, a woman described a hand-washing compulsion, and her analyst interpreted her behavior as a symbolic attempt to rid herself of guilt feelings regarding adulterous behavior. A somewhat less Freudian example involved a counselor's interpretation of a woman's habitual failure to pass a driving test. The counselor interpreted this as an attempt to maintain a dependent relationship with her husband because of her suppressed fear of losing him if he felt she could get along by herself.

The use of interpretation as a depth technique should be based on understanding of the system of constructs on which it is based. A basic contention underlying this book is that such an orientation is needlessly involved and inappropriate for secondary school counselors. It follows, then, that in the frame of reference suggested here for secondary school counseling, depth interpretation should not be used.

There is, however, a sense in which a kind of interpretation can be used effectively by high school counselors as a technique for helping students solve their problems. The idea that students often do not see the implications of their remarks has been mentioned before. In counseling we typically do not spell out these implications for students, but rather, attempt to help students perceive them for themselves. However, there are occasions when much time can be saved in interpreting the significance of a statement, with sacrificing meaning for the student. The following excerpt illustrates this point.

C: Can you think of any other reasons?

S: Well, some kids dislike me, and I can't say I blame them. The kids in the social club would just as soon have me whacked into little bits and fed to the sharks.

C: Do you think there could be some element of jealously here?

S: I retreat. In fact about the only time I go on the offensive in an attack is if someone else is involved, but if it's me I go back. I've heard Mom say that I put on sort of a crutch going to school and I actually do. It's a lot easier. But if I get mad many times my world would shatter and then it would be too easy for them to do it again. I've had that happen a couple of times. I had a friend once who was a very good friend of mine, and she became involved in the social regime and having me for a friend didn't work, and so she politely, if you want to call it politely, told me that I was a social risk, ta, ta. And we haven't spoken much since then. She's at the top of the social ladder now.

C: Have you ever thought that this might be something you might grow out of? When you get out of high school and go to college that this won't be the big problem it is now? With a different group?

S: Well, I think when the group is changed it may not be so bad. I don't have the same trouble when I'm around the players, but it's different because everyone has developed respect for everyone else. Most of the people there are fairly sensitive.

The same caution mentioned in regard to other techniques toward this end of the leading continuum is appropriate here. Regardless of how logical and valid the counselor's interpretation may be, the student must be ready to understand and accept it before it can have a positive influence. Otherwise, the interpretation is likely to be meaningless, confusing, or threatening to the student.

## Advice

The next technique listed on the leading continuum is advice. It should be obvious by this point that a real distinction is made in this book between counseling and advising. There are those, however, who equate the two. The assumption is made that because the counselor is older, more mature, wiser, and so on, his appropriate function is to tell the student what to do. There are others who feel that advice has absolutely no place in counseling. The position taken here is somewhere near the latter extreme. Occasionally situations arise in counseling in which the counselor has every reason to believe that the student is about to engage in behavior that will have significantly undesirable effects for himself or others. For example, a pregnant high school girl may reveal plans to leave the community and seek the services of an abortionist in a large city. A boy may indicate that he plans to run away from home. In cases such as these, when the counselor believes that the student will carry out his plan, advice would seem appropriate, assuming, of course, that the counselor has reason to believe that *the counselee will accept his advice.*

More frequently a student may request advice of less dramatic nature. For example, he may want to know whether he should take both the College Board aptitude and achievement tests or just the aptitude test, or whether to apply to his second choice college before or after hearing from his first choice, or whether to report what he knows about a school theft to the principal or the dean. Often the help can be provided by supplying advice, but letting the student take responsibility for the actual decision.

## Rejection

The last technique listed on the continuum is rejection. When employing this technique the counselor openly and forcefully directs the session to a consideration of his own feelings.

S: So, as far as I can see there is no point in my staying in school any longer.
C: But there is! You need an education. . . .

The distinction should be made between rejecting a counselee or his statements and feelings without being aware of the rejection, and using rejection as a counseling technique. In the former situation the counselor has most probably lost all perspective on the interview and on his function as a counselor. When used purposefully, rejection is an attempt to give extremely strong support or reassurance to the assertion opposite to the one expressed by the student. While purposeful rejection can appear to have a desirable influence on the counselee, the behavior change is largely limited to the verbal level, and rather short-lived at that. Perhaps what actually happens is that the student becomes inhibited enough by the rejection from the counselor (whom he now perceives as a definite authority figure) that he reacts as he would to authority figures in noncounseling situations. Once removed from the situation, he no longer needs to maintain the appearance of agreeing with the counselor.

## SUMMARY

The techniques discussed in this chapter exist as categories rather than methods. The illustrations presented should have made this clear. Also, the continuum of lead upon which the techniques have been placed is an abstraction, a construct employed to help the reader understand the material presented. No assumptions have been made about the distance between techniques on the continuum. Nor can it be argued that the techniques have been placed in exactly the correct sequence. The techniques themselves are abstractions. Counselors may respond to a student in a manner similar to what has been labeled clarification, for instance, but what each counselor actually does depends on his own state at a particular time and also on that of the particular counselee. In other words, the classification of counselor responses according to the continuum of lead is not nearly as precise as a classification of people according to weight or height, but it is a classification which provides a better understanding of the counseling process than would be possible without it.

### Suggested References

McKinney, Fred, *Counseling for Personal Adjustment,* Houghton Mifflin, 1958.

A great variety of counseling cases are presented in this volume. Most examples involve college students, but there are pertinent implications for counseling in secondary schools. Counseling techniques are also illustrated in numerous sections of the book.

Patterson, C. H., "Implementing the Point of View," in *Counseling and Psychotherapy,* Harper, 1959, chap. 8.

Robinson, Francis P., "Dimensions and Techniques in Counseling," "Immediate Criteria in Counseling," and "The Effectiveness of Counseling Techniques," in *Principles and Procedures in Student Counseling,* Harper, 1950, chaps. IV, V, VI.

Rogers, Carl R., "Old and New Viewpoints in Counseling and Psychotherapy," in *Counseling and Psychotherapy,* Houghton Mifflin, 1942, chap. II.

# CHAPTER 6

....................................................................................

# Frequent Counseling Tasks

---

Although it is desirable for the counselor to keep in mind that each counselee is unique and thus should not be treated just like any other, it is also observable that counselees show certain similarities. With these similarities this chapter is concerned. They can be viewed as counseling tasks which transcend the various school counseling contexts suggested in Chapter 1. They develop more frequently within some contexts than in others, but to some extent the secondary school counselor will be faced with them in each of the counseling contexts suggested. The counseling tasks, in order of consideration, are information giving, interpreting test results, dealing with hostility during counseling, referrals, and parent conferences.

The counselor needs to relate these tasks to his counseling frame of reference. The counselor, in other words, should have a rationale for each of these tasks. For example, he should have certain purposes in giving educational information, and these purposes should serve to determine the methods he employs to give information to counselees. The purpose of this chapter, then, is to relate each of the counseling tasks to the frame of reference suggested in Chapter 2. Only incidental attention will be given to the knowledges and specific procedures necessary in accomplishing these tasks. References to sources of specific discussions of these matters have been listed at the end of the chapter.

## INFORMATION GIVING

It is obvious that to make appropriate decisions about his current situation and about his future, the adolescent needs many kinds of information. What should be almost as obvious is that the possession of relevant information does not necessarily result in appropriate decisions. There is a difference, as was pointed out earlier, between understanding and accepting information. This difference should be emphasized in the information-giving tasks of counseling. Much of the information that students need to possess in order to make appropriate decisions is acquired through the day-to-day informal experiences of living. Of course, a great deal of general environmental information has been organized and is somewhat formally presented to students through academic courses. In addition, most guidance programs go a step further and organize relatively specific information needed by secondary school students in their attempts to make vocational, educational, and personal decisions. Therefore, for the most part, the school counselor need devote little counseling time to giving information.

As an information-giving function of guidance, counseling should be concerned, first, with helping the student accept information and integrate it into his own system of personal assertions; second, with helping students understand information already made available to them; and third, with presenting information which is new to the student. Students should come to planning interviews having studied whatever information is indicated. Obviously, the counselor cannot predict precisely what information will be needed, nor can he always make adequate reference to information sources, nor assume that students will acquire the information. So, the three steps suggested make up a kind of continuum of desirable emphases for the task of information giving in counseling. The following example should illustrate the point.

Harry attended several group guidance meetings devoted to college admission requirements. General considerations were explained and sources of information were discussed. The counselor had prepared several exercises illustrating information-getting problems. The students used college catalogues, occupational briefs, and other materials to solve the information problems and then discussed the uses and limitations of the sources with the counselor. Following the meetings, counseling interviews were scheduled with those students interested in working through college plans. The counselor emphasized that students should use the information sources available and secure whatever information they thought they would need during the counseling session. Many students were able to secure pertinent information prior to counseling. Some came with only partial information and were given some specific references to use before their next interviews. Harry was one of the students in the latter group. However, when he arrived for the second counseling session, the counselor discovered that Harry had failed to use the references and was still without adequate information.

Now, if the continuum of emphases suggested above had been followed implicitly, the counselor again would have referred Harry to information sources. There are other considerations, however. Perhaps the most important is the fact that a definite amount of time had been reserved for Harry. Consequently, if the counselor believed that Harry's problems could not be discussed meaningfully on the basis of the information Harry possessed, he might well have decided to spend a few minutes giving information. In terms of the continuum of desirable emphases, this would not represent effective use of counseling time. Viewing the problem more broadly, however, we recognize that failure to provide the information then and there might result in even less effective use of counseling time.

Other situations arise where students cannot find information, or where information is available but inappropriately arranged for a specific purpose. Consider the following illustration.

Anna was about to complete the first semester of her junior year in high school. She was a very bright girl with considerable social sophistication. She and her parents had developed interest in the early admissions program at a liberal arts college. Because she had completed extra units towards high school graduation, she felt that she might have enough credits for graduation by the end of her junior year. She and her parents wanted specific information on the high school's early graduation policy, as well as on the implications of an early admission program. The counselor, and the girl, and her parents to a lesser degree, realized that the lack of information was only one aspect of the problem. Yet, the information was essential to solving the problem, and it had to be obtained and organized according to the unique requirements of the situation. It is apparent, then, that secondary school counselors sometimes need to devote counseling time to giving information. Nevertheless, school counselors can and should use economical methods for providing information so that information giving during counseling time itself can be kept to a minimum.

Thus far we have been discussing aspects of providing information. Now what are some considerations involved in helping students accept information? Perhaps a more basic question is, why do students need help in accepting information? There are at least two reasons. First, students actually may not understand information sufficiently to perceive its personal significance. Second, the information, even when sufficiently understood, may offer serious disconfirmations. As a result, accepting the information may be perceived as entailing unpleasant changes in plans, attitudes, or aspirations. If the changes are perceived as being sufficiently unpleasant, the student can protect himself by simply refusing to accept the information. Failure to understand information and perceive disconfirmations are not unrelated, of course. They are often interactive, and solving one problem can operate to minimize the other.

The following two examples illustrate problems in accepting information. The first is a case of inadequate understanding inhibiting acceptance of information, and the second is one of understood information entailing serious disconfirmations. Both examples point up the interaction between the two causes of nonacceptance of information. Following the illustrations are general suggestions on what the counselor can do to help students accept information.

Towards the end of her sophomore year in high school, Betty was scheduled to meet with her counselor for the purpose of reviewing her educational plans. Personal data in her cumulative folder indicated that her vocational goal was nursing. She had taken college preparation courses in anticipation of enrolling in the college of nursing at the state university. She had completed both algebra and biology during her freshman and sophomore years, receiving D's in both courses. Both teachers involved had made comments in Betty's cumulative folder to the effect that her achievement grades should have been F's, and that the passing grades of D reflected her diligent efforts and cooperative attitude.

The counselor had made notes of previous educational planning sessions with Betty. These served to remind him that the appropriateness of her vocational goal had been considered at the beginning of Grade 10. Betty had been given information on nursing schools, and she and the counselor had discussed the requirements of the several types of nursing programs. All of the evidence possessed by the counselor suggested that there was little chance of Betty's being admitted to a college or university department of nursing. Her chances of being admitted to a three-year program, while a little better, also seemed very poor. The possibility of her being admitted to a one-year practical nursing program at the state university was very good. The latter program did not have high school algebra and science as prerequisites.

Because Betty had read and discussed this information, the counselor was puzzled when she stated her intention to take chemistry in her junior year and physics in her senior year. An excerpt from the ensuing counseling follows.

C: How do your vocational goals stand now, Betty?

S: Just the same. Being a nurse is still what I want to do.

C: I see, and you have been taking the courses which you will need to get into a college of nursing. I also see that you plan to take chemistry next year.

S: Yes. The nursing school catalogues say that you don't have to have it but that it helps. Since I don't do real well in science and math, I thought that I should take as many courses in it as I can.

C: You feel that you can make up for not doing so well in biology by taking chemistry and physics.

S: Yes, I hope so at least.

C: This is related to what we talked about at the first of the year. Betty, would you like to review the discussion we had at that time?

S: Okay.

C: What do you recall from that talk?

S: Well, let's see, we—uh—you told me about requirements for being a nurse, and about different kinds of nurses.

C: Yes, we talked about various requirements for being admitted to nursing school. How did you feel you stood, in terms of getting into a school?

S: I remember you said that my test scores and grades should improve, or I might have trouble.

C: Yes.

(*Pause.*)

S: Well, I guess they haven't, but that's why I'm going to take more science. I should do better now that I've had biology.

C: We're back to that point again, aren't we, Betty? You feel that if you just stay with it long enough, you'll understand it.

S: It is very discouraging. But how else can I be a nurse?

C: We talked about three kinds of nursing programs. Do you remember? The degree program, the diploma program, and the program leading to graduation as a certified practical nurse?

S: I remember, but I guess I don't really think that the last one you mentioned is a nurse. My mother says that a practical nurse is like a nurse's aid, or just a woman who helps out. That's not really a nurse.

C: It's important that you be more than that, isn't it? You want to feel that you have some training and are recognized as being able to do a regular job in a hospital or clinic?

S: Yes, that's right.

C: Would you like to take another look at this certified practical nurse idea? There may be more to it than you see.

S: Okay.

C: Well, first, what does the word *certified* mean to you?

S: It, oh . . . well . . . I don't really know, I guess. What does it mean?

C: In this case, Betty, it means that the state has set up certain qualifications for being a practical nurse—just as they have set up qualifications for other occupations, such as doctors, teachers, electricians, beauty operators, dentists, and so forth. Colleges or hospitals offering practical nursing courses train students so that they can meet the necessary qualifications. After students have the training and have passed the state examination, they are given a state certificate which allows them to be employed as a certified practical nurse. Because practical nurses have less training, they do not do all of the things that registered nurses do. There are differences, but there are also many similarities. They work in hospitals as trained and certified people.

S: Gee! I didn't understand. What do you have to take to get into a certified practical nurse program?

C: Before you leave I'll give you the folder that you saw at the first of the year which describes the program. In general, you need to be a high school graduate. General math and general science would satisfy entrance requirements.

The actual interview with Betty was somewhat longer and more time was spent on description of the work of a certified practical nurse. It also included discussion of the influence on Betty's assertions of a change of plans from being a registered nurse to being a certified practical nurse. The limited excerpt, however, illustrates the point that failure to accept information can be the result of failure to understand the information. The counselor could have taken a different approach than he did. For example, he could have assumed that Betty's persistence in preparing to become a registered nurse, in spite of her failures, was due to the disconfirmations involved in giving up her goal: being anything "less" than a nurse meant giving up assertions about ability and desired status, a prospect which was painful. As it was, however, checking out the possibility of failure to understand information paid off. This is often true, and thus attention to decreasing ambiguity by straightforward help in understanding information can be important.

In terms of the proposed frame of reference, the counselor in such a case is attempting to help the counselee clarify the relationships between assertions and behavior resulting from assertions. It is very possible that by doing this the counselor sets the stage for perceived disconfirmations. In other words, as long as a certain amount of ambiguity about an assertion exists, a student may quite honestly fail to see the disconfirming implications of his behavior, and thus follow inadequate patterns of behavior. Decreasing the ambiguity surrounding the relationship can make the situation temporarily worse, as when the student perceives the probable inadequacy (disconfirming nature) of his proposed behavior. It is then up to the counselor to help the student develop revised assertions by accepting the information according to the increased understanding.

There are times, however, when there is very little ambiguity about pertinent information. The student has achieved an adequate understanding of the facts, but is still unable to accept the information. Two examples of students unable to accept situations because of the disconfirmations involved were given in Chapter 4. The following is an example of a student unable to accept specific information.

Dale was a high school senior planning to enter the Air Force after high school graduation. He had read Air Force occupational briefs and talked to Air Force recruiters and to his counselor about his plans. He had even made preliminary arrangements to enter the service, and hoped to be placed in one of three Air Force technical schools. He understood that the actual school would be determined after he enlisted. His original plan was to enter preflight school, but under existing conditions this was impossible without at least two years of college and quite improbable without four years. Dale had read these regulations and had discussed the situation with the Air Force recruiter and his counselor. Both felt that Dale had accepted the information and had changed his plans accordingly.

The counselor was surprised, then, when the Air Force recruiter called and asked for an appointment to discuss Dale's enlistment. The recruiter met with the counselor and described the following situation. Dale had arrived at the recruiting office to complete some enlistment forms and had stated that he was anxious to enter preflight training. The recruiter reminded Dale that this was impossible, and that he thought that Dale understood the regulations. Dale said that he understood but that he was sure that once he got in the Air Force he would be able to convince people that he had the necessary interest for becoming a pilot. The recruiter pointed out that interest was irrelevant in his case, but Dale's optimism was not to be shaken. The recruiter managed to defer the completion of the forms and contacted the counselor.

The counselor agreed to see Dale. The following excerpt approximates part of the interview.

C:  Sergeant Helm asked me to see you about your Air Force plans, Dale. He thought that you might not completely understand some of the facts involved. Would you like to talk about it for a few minutes?

S:  Okay. What's wrong?

C:  I'm not sure that anything is wrong, but I wonder if you understand the regulations concerning preflight school.

S:  Sure: The regulations say that I have to have at least two years of college to get in. Isn't that right?

C:  Yes, that's right. What effect do you feel that this rule will have on you?

S:  Well, obviously I won't have two years of college. According to the rules, I can't be a pilot.

C:  You see a way around the rules, perhaps.

S:  I think that when I get in and have a chance to talk to somebody besides the sergeant, and show them how interested I am, they'll let me in.

C:  I see. Let's just suppose for a minute that they wouldn't let you in, and that you would be enrolled in a technical school after basic training. How would you feel about that?

S:  I wouldn't stay in.
    (*Pause.*)

C:  You wouldn't stay in.

S:  No. I'd get out. Get discharged some way. I want to be a pilot, not a mechanic or something.

C:  Well, if this were to happen, that is, you found yourself in the Air Force and wanted to get out, it might be somewhat unpleasant for you, don't you think?

S:  Yes.

C:  Maybe you could avoid this problem by talking about a few things. Can you tell me why you feel so strongly about being a pilot?

After a few general statements, Dale began to describe his situation. He revealed an intense need to be respected by his peers. As he progressed through high school, his friends began to discuss post-high-school plans. As a sophomore, Dale announced his intention to become an Air Force pilot. By the end of his junior year he had committed himself to a career as an Air Force pilot, and perceived his stated plans as bringing him his friends' respect. The respect confirmed positive assertions about his importance, and for the first time that he could recall, he felt that he was accepted. He had reasoned that giving up his pilot plans would have lost him his newly gained respect, and the predicted disconfirmation was too painful to accept. His redundant behavior resulted from the tension and conflict produced by the Air Force information. The counselor helped Dale to clarify the relationship between his assertions and his vocational plans, and then it became possible for Dale to accept the Air Force regulations, as discouraging as they were, and to begin making realistic decisions.

The references at the end of this chapter suggest useful sources of the various kinds of information provided by guidance programs, as well as counseling and noncounseling means for communicating the information to students. The following considerations for dealing with the information problem during counseling summarize briefly what has been discussed in this section. It should be remembered that exceptions exist for each generalization.

1. Environmental information in counseling should be employed with purpose and discrimination. Assuming appropriate noncounseling means of providing information have been used, specific rather than general references to information sources should be made to counselees. It must be assumed that counselees are sufficiently familiar with occupational information files to use them easily.

2. The counselor should use only information sources with which he is familiar, during actual counseling. That, he should not use sources for the first time during counseling. A very effective means of destroying rapport and losing a counselee's confidence is for the counselor to pick up an occupational brief or two and fail to find what he just said he could find.

3. In order to provide for limitations of information sources, students should be referred to several sources, or to an information file containing several sources.

4. Environmental information should be used to help the counselee increase his knowledge, not to prove the counselor's point. Often the information does tend to prove the counselor's point, but every attempt should be made to keep this outcome incidental to the primary purpose. Counseling turns rapidly into advising and argumentative conversation when points need to be proved.

5. It is important to get feedback from the counselee about his understanding of the information and its influence on his assertions. Understanding is relatively easy for the alert counselor to perceive, but the influence of newly gained environmental information on a student's assertions is often less obvious.

6. The counselor should attempt to identify and remember his own

biases when using occupational information in counseling. If the counselor believes that he needs to evaluate information for a student, the evaluation should be labeled as such.

## TEST INTERPRETATION

While we certainly do not know everything regarding the measurement of psychological characteristics, we have come a long way in learning what questions to ask. The relatively recent work in educational and psychological measurement is reflected in both the increased certainty and the increased caution with which educational and psychological practitioners employ test results. Operational relationships have been established between various kinds of test results and ensuing behavior. Given certain test data about an individual, we know the probability of his behaving in certain ways. Thus we are able to do an increasingly more satisfactory job of occupational and educational selection, and of identifying people in need of the various kinds of educational and psychotherapeutic treatment.

At the same time we have come to recognize the complexities of psychological characteristics. Intelligence, for example, is an ambiguous term. One must ask, intelligence by what criterion? Do we mean one's score on a test, or one's rate of learning, or how much one can learn, or the extent to which one can apply what he had learned? Or do we mean several of these things at once? If so, in what proportions and in what ways do we combine these several meanings? Perhaps an even more difficult question, once we have defined a characteristic called intelligence, is, in what ways is it tempered by other characteristics of an individual and by environmental conditions within which he must operate?

If this much ambiguity exists in regard to intelligence, about which, along with achievement, we often talk with much apparent certainty, then what can we do about admittedly more nebulous characteristics in the areas of interest and personality? The suggestion is not being made here that the counselor should avoid using educational and psychological tests until they are perfected. Psychological measuring instruments in their current status are an invaluable counseling tool. It was pointed out in a previous chapter that in order to help his counselees systematically the counselor needs information about them. Tests and nontest appraisal instruments represent the primary method of securing this information. In order to use tests effectively and meaningfully in counseling, the counselor must (1) possess technical information about tests, (2) understand assumptions involved in test construction, (3) be aware of available tests, what they are designed to measure, and how well they accomplish their purposes, and (4) develop a rationale for using test results in counseling.

It is the fourth requirement with which this section is concerned. First, however, let it be said that the second requirement is a means and not an end in itself. The high school counselor need not be a test construction expert. His job is not to develop tests, but rather to use tests developed by others. It is obvious, however, that a necessary condition of being able to use tests intelligently, that is, to be aware of available tests, what they are designed to measure, and how well they accomplish their purposes, is an understanding of how tests are developed. For example, to know that a test should be reliable is not enough. It is important that the counselor be aware that reliability is not only a function of the test itself, but also of the manner in which it is computed and of the nature of the norm groups involved. The high school counselor's preparation should include instruction in these areas. As a practicing counselor he should strive for continued sophistication in the development and use of psychological and educational measuring instruments. Several testing references are provided at the end of this chapter. These by themselves are not adequate for the kind of understanding suggested above, but they have been found to be excellent sources for use by counselors with limited preparation and in immediate need of a better understanding of testing.

Like environmental information, test results should be used with a purpose in counseling. The rationale which follows aims to provide such purpose. Some students may be disappointed in the general nature of what follows and wish for a rather definite set or rules. These are indeed desirable, but cannot be supplied at present. For every rule one could cite, there would be many important exceptions. One can develop, however, some generalizations which will facilitate specific decisions about the use of test results. The following statements have proved useful to counselors in training. As the reader gains counseling experience he may want to modify, augment, or even reject them. An underlying assumption is that most testing in secondary schools is mass testing; with few exceptions, the high school counselor has similar test data on all of his counselees. The rationale, then, is primarily one for the use of test results, rather than for the selection of tests to be administered.

1. While test results have many uses, they can all be viewed as fostering students' ability to predict future behavior and circumstances, and thus make appropriate decisions. In the case of achievement and scholastic aptitude tests, the point is rather obvious. When, for instance, a student knows the relationship between his scores on the Iowa Test of Educational Development and his chances for admission to various colleges, he should be able to make a more appropriate decision about seeking entrance to colleges than he can without the knowledge. The same concept can be applied, though less clearly, perhaps, to valid measures of personality and interest. For example, while knowing his pattern on the Strong Interest Inventory may increase a student's self-understanding, it is the use of the self-understanding that counts. Knowing his interest patterns and what they mean should enable him to make more accurate and meaningful predictions, which in turn should facilitate making decisions. Similarly, a personality measurement suggesting that one tends to be a highly dominant individual provides information that allows more accurate prediction of the appropriateness of various kinds of jobs than would be possible without the information.

Test results are also used to build up students' self-confidence. In terms of our frame of reference, the counselor is helping the student to clarify his assertions, and in this sense uses test results as a means of confirming appropriate assertions. Thus, indirectly, the test data facilitate more accurate predictions and decision making.

2. Reporting test results should increase a student's knowledge of himself. It follows that test results should not be reported when a student obviously possesses the same information from some other source, or alternatively, test results which duplicate existing information should be reported in such a way as to add to a student's appreciation of the relationship between the information and other phenomena. For example, take the case of a student who has scored below the 15th percentile on both a standardized achievement test and a test of scholastic aptitude at the beginning of her senior year in high school. Assuming expected achievement during her high school career, the suggestion that the counselor explain to the girl that her achievement and scholastic apti-

tude score are at or above that of 15 percent of such and such a population is inappropriate. Similarly, it is ridiculous to tell a bright, high-achieving, self-confident student planning to attend college that his scholastic aptitude score is within the top 5 percent of all scores. In neither case is the knowledge news, nor is it of much use to the students. What is of use, however, as shown even in these over-simplified examples, is to report the results in such a way as to significantly help the student make decisions. The counselor may be able to help the girl (who has probably experienced consistent failure throughout her school career) predict occupational areas in which she might be relatively successful. The boy may be having difficulty deciding on a college. The test results can be reported in such a way as to help him with his decision. It is up to the counselor, then, to translate test data into information which will be helpful and meaningful to students, if the information is needed. If the boy referred to above had selected an appropriate college, there would be little point in even calling the test results to his attention.

3. Because of the many possibilities for misunderstanding test results, the counselee's perception of the meaning of reported test data should be appraised. This point of feedback has been discussed in general and at some length in previous chapters. It has special applicability to reporting test data. By securing feedback from the student the counselor can gauge the counselee's understanding of the information, the extent to which selective perception is operating, and the effect of the information on the student's assertions. The procedure is a simple one. Questions such as "Now, will you tell me in your own words what this means to you," "How do you feel about these results," or "How do these results influence your decisions and plans," usually secure the desired feedback.

4. Students should be given opportunities, prior to counseling, to develop realistic ideas of what they can expect to find out from test results. They should also be given opportunities to learn any particular terms and concepts which the counselor expects to use in interpreting test results. Some schools offer effective guidance units during the student's first year in the school to provide this kind of preparation. Other schools hold series of special meetings with students prior to counseling, and still others integrate such material into regular courses, such as mathematics. Whatever the method, many communication problems

regarding test results in counseling can be anticipated by some form of systematic preparation.

## HOSTILITY DURING COUNSELING

Counselee hostility towards the counselor and counseling is another kind of situation which transcends the various counseling contexts. The problem may be of lesser importance to secondary school counselors than to counselors in other situations, but it occurs frequently enough in some degree to merit comment here.

What should the counselor do about counselee hostility? In brief, he should recognize it and encourage the student to do the same. Counselee hostility can be a result of a number of variables. Perhaps two of the most frequent causes of hostility are what depth-oriented therapists refer to as transference and counter-transference. Exposition of the total meanings and implications of these terms would be needlessly complex for our purposes, but a general notion of each is useful. Transference, very generally, refers to the counselee's attributing characteristics of some other person to the counselor. Thus, a girl who has certain negative percepts of various characteristics of her father may transfer these percepts and the hostility associated with them from her father to her counselor. Counter-transference is similar, except that here the counselor is doing the transfering. As a result of behavior by the counselor based on transference, the counselee may quite logically (or psychologically) react to the counselor as he does to persons in his intimate environment.

There are other sources of hostility in counseling. These, as well as the one just described, can be accounted for in terms of the frame of reference suggested earlier. Students can perceive all kinds of situations to have disconfirming influences on their assertions. It should not be the least bit surprising, then, to find the counseling relationship and the counselor perceived in a similar way. As a matter of fact, it would be very surprising indeed if some students did *not* perceive counseling in such a way. After all, counseling is a situation in which the student is often invited to discuss the very things he has been avoiding for some time. Regardless of what the real cause of the hostility may be, if it is directed toward the counselor, then counseling is the appropriate place from which it should be viewed. The counselor is relatively certain that it exists then and there in relation to a given topic. He is relatively uncertain of causes which might be inferred. Further, it is more important to emphasize the operational than the causal significance of hostility. Operationally, hostility can be viewed as inhibiting effective counseling or as a counselee problem to which it is appropriate to devote counseling attention, or both.

As to method, an honest straightforward approach is suggested. One may say, "Talking about this seems to make you a little anxious; would you like to tell me why?" or, "Telling me these things is not easy, and you feel some resentment towards me for having asked you these things, don't you?" This will often suffice to open the topic of hostility for frank discussion. Any attempt to cover up the hostility, or to approach it without actually admitting that it exists, carries the very real possibility of reinforcing the counselee's reluctance to discuss his feelings. If the counselor is unwilling to be frank and honest then the counselee is likely to be so also.

Beginning counselors have raised the question of whether or not dealing with hostility in an interview scheduled for some specific purpose, such as educational planning, is a desirable direction for the interview to take. "Won't this tend to keep the student from talking about his real problem?" they say. "Why not help him with the stated purpose of the counseling session and defer the hostility problem to a later time?" There is a certain logic in this suggestion as long as one assumes that different stated problems are in fact separate and distinct. The point of view taken in this book, as stated previously, is that this assumption is in no way valid. Labeling problems is an extremely high level of abstraction. A problem represents a certain combination of characteristics within a given set of circumstances. An underachiever in high school A, for example, might not be an underachiever in high school B. A juvenile delinquent under California law may not be a juvenile delinquent under Florida law. A student with an apprenticeship placement problem under condition X may not have the problem under condition Y. Thus, hostility in counseling should be viewed as a circumstance pertinent to the problem being discussed and the existing counseling relationship. It should be of immediate concern because of its probable negative influence on the counseling session. In other words, it makes little sense for a counselor to continue counseling with a hostile student without first attempting to clear up the hostility. With some students this may involve demonstrating what happens in counseling as well as discussing the hostility. With other students it may involve changing counselors, or even terminating counseling.

## REFERRALS

The school counselor sometimes finds that he can best serve a student by referring him to other school personnel or to personnel in non-school agencies. As a matter of fact, if a school counselor believes that he has a responsibility to all students, then referrals become almost a necessity. The counselor works with students who have a great variety and complexity of problems. He attempts to help the majority of these youngsters through relatively short-term counseling. Actually, he cannot afford to devote large amounts of time to some of his counselees if he expects to spend some time with each of them. Even if he could involve students with atypical needs in long-term counseling or some other form of assistance, he often lacks the training and experience to be as effective as various specialists available to his counselees. In some cases there is also the question of the extent to which the counselor, as a representative of the school, should provide therapy.

School counselors often report frustrations in their referral efforts. Too often the referral process fails to provide anticipated results. Parents, teachers, counselors, and students are disappointed, or even aggravated, over events in a given referral. Thus school counselors ask, "How do you make an effective referral—one that is beneficial to all persons involved?" For this, as for other questions discussed in this book, there is no formula or universal answer. Perhaps, however, a rationale can be suggested which will aid the counselor in decisions and actions with students for whom referrals are contemplated.

The term *referral* can be used to describe what one does to a student, or to designate a process in which one involves a student. The distinction is an important one, and the latter use is to be preferred. The first use suggests a kind of transfer of the counselee from one person to another. In some professional areas this may be a fairly adequate description of what appropriately takes place when a referral is made. Within the context of secondary school counseling, it is not an appropriate description. With a few exceptions, students who are referred by counselors to some other person or agency continue to spend a large portion of their time in school. A school's responsibilities to a student do not cease with a referral. Often, as a matter of fact, they become greater and more complex after a referral has been initiated. Instead of transferring responsibility, the counselor most frequently helps a counselee obtain assistance or services which he, the counselor, is unable to provide. The assistance or services may be relatively distinct from those of the counselor and the school, or as is most often the case, may be related.

At one extreme, for example, would be a student who indicated simply a desire to discuss a conflict in religious ideologies. A relatively bright, normal high school senior was extremely interested in enrolling in a college supported and administered by a religious group which held beliefs considerably different from his own. He had a frank and honest desire to learn whether the religious difference might result in embarrassment and discomfort for him. The boy's own minister had been unable to help him, and the counselor felt he did not have the required information. However, the counselor knew a clergyman connected with the church administering the school in question who could provide an objective estimate of the circumstances that might develop. The counselor helped initiate the referral. His only other involvement was when the student reported that he had talked with the clergyman and had obtained the information he sought.

At the other extreme would be a student manifesting a problem with medical, psychological, familial, and economic ramifications. In such a case, the counselor, over a year's time, helped the student secure aid from a medical practicioner, a school psychologist, a social welfare agency, and the local employment service. The student remained in school, and in addition to using the above services, met with the counselor for three or four sessions. The counselor was in contact with the nonschool personnel as well as the parents and school personnel. Primary responsibility lay in different hands from time to time, but at all times all persons concerned worked together in the student's interest. In both of these illustrations the students remained in school. Examples of referrals resulting in a student's being removed from school temporarily or permanently could be described. These are rare, however. From the school counselor's perspective, it is more sensible to think of referrals as a means of securing help for students while they continue to attend school.

It is not uncommon to hear secondary school administrators advise their counseling staffs that school counselors are not psychological counselors, and that they should therefore be extremely careful to avoid discussing "psychological problems" with students. Further, school counselors are often told that they do have a responsibility to identify students with psychological problems. Having identified such students, they are to refer them to "someone who knows how to deal with such things." Would it were that simple! Our present purpose is not to define the role of school counselors, but it seems pertinent in passing to suggest that school counseling, by definition, is "psychological," as is all counseling in the professional sense. To suggest that school counselors avoid psychological problem areas in counseling is ridiculous. The extreme caution recommended to counselors, as described above, is necessary only when the counselors are faculty members lacking in professional preparation for their counseling assignments. It is not school counselors who should be cautioned, but rather school administrators who assign counseling responsibilities to teachers who lack adquate preparation for them. Although many school administrators are aware of this problem, the attitude described above toward the use of referral sources is fairly common. If counselors are adequately prepared, a procedure of automatic referrals can result in greater harm to students than will be done by restricting help to that available within a school system. All appropriate and dependable sources of aid should be employed. In other words, while it is important for counselors to know how to make referrals, it is even more important that they know when to make them.

The discussion which follows should not be interpreted as a check list for referrals. It most emphatically is not one. Nevertheless, the steps that may well lead to a referral decision can be considered under three headings: (1) generally considering whether or not to refer a student, (2) determining the nature of a particular referral, and (3) implementing a specific referral. The classification, as a basis for operation, is somewhat arbitrary, but it should serve the purposes of discussion.

The basic decision to refer a student or not involves at least six factors. These will not necessarily be given in order of importance. First, the school policy on referrals must be considered. A counselor should work within the policies of his particular school system. If the policy is not to refer students directly, there is little point in initiating a referral process. Schools vary in the extent to which they choose to become involved with nonschool agencies. Some schools communicate information to parents and then attempt to divorce themselves from further referral responsibilities. Regardless of how a counselor feels about his system's policy, and regardless of what he may be doing to influence policy changes constructively, he should understand and work within existing policy. To do otherwise is to destroy administrative support.

A second factor which should influence a referral decision is the counselor's own professional competencies as related to a given student and the nature of his problems. It seems only reasonable to believe that a counselor with a year or more of graduate preparation and counseling experience should have some psychological counseling competencies.

A third factor is the amount of counseling time available. Even though he has adequate counseling competencies, the counselor may feel that he is not justified in giving large amounts of time to one student to the neglect of others. Not all potential referral cases require large amounts of counseling time, but many of them do.

A fourth consideration is the availability of appropriate referral sources. Counselors need more information about referral agencies than may be given in a descriptive brochure, since the interests, facilities, and adequacy of various agencies differ tremendously. For example, social welfare agencies vary from those employing highly trained and competent social workers to those staffed by one trained supervisor assisted by a corps of well-intentioned but totally untrained caseworkers. In many areas of the country, agencies are forced into the latter position because professional personnel is not available. Such agencies need not be condemned; many of them are very effective. It is appropriate, however, that school counselors know the nature of agencies in their communities, so that they can make purposeful referrals within predictable positive limits. In regard to other referral sources and personnel there is the same need for awareness. All psychiatrists, for example, do not work equally well with adolescents. Some are in fact very ineffective with high school youngsters who are neither neurotic nor psychotic. Usually professional workers and adequately staffed agencies respond very frankly to counselors' inquiries about the nature of their services. They too are anxious to prevent inappropriate referrals.

A fifth factor in a referral decision is the probable effect of a referral on the student (as far as it can be predicted). This point obviously overlaps others already mentioned, but it is important and to some extent separate. The counselor should ask himself what will probably happen to a student both by design and incidentally, if referral sources are utilized. The prediction is of course difficult to make—at least with adequate precision. However, it is worthwhile attempting if only in terms of possible incidental influences. For example, what may be the influence on family or home life of referral to a vocational rehabilitation agency? What peer-group reactions may develop if a student is referred to a local mental hygiene clinic? Often considerations of this type will not prevent a decision to refer, but may suggest additional provisions that should be made in the referral process.

The sixth factor which needs to be considered in a referral decision is the attitude of the student towards a specific referral action. A universal belief in the teaching and helping professions is that motivation is a necessary condition for changing behavior. There is little value in referring a counselee to other sources of help if he does not want them. One need not give up, however, when a counselee refuses to accept outside help. By offering information, support, and greater self-understanding, the counselor can often interfere with a counselee's motivation not to receive referral help. The school counselor should seldom find it necessary to refer a student without first obtaining the student's permission. The exceptional cases are most often those in which the school has a legal responsibility to make the referral.

Once the desirability of utilizing referral aid has been established, the counselor must decide on the nature of a particular referral. Two factors should be considered. First, what degree of referral is desirable? This is a question of the extent to which the student is to be involved with the referral source. The possible extremes have been described earlier in this chapter. Often the question is wholly determined by the policy of the referral source. Many times a student's reluctance to accept referral help can influence this determination. The problem of the degree of referral necessarily is influenced by other factors mentioned above, such as the competencies of the counselor and the rapport between the student and the counselor. The following examples illustrate this point.

Otto was a senior in high school who manifested extremely ineffective academic and social behavior. His school counselor had developed several hypotheses on the nature of his problems but wanted further data to validate and extend his "diagnosis." A mental health clinic was available and could provide the needed help. The question arose of the extent to which the clinic should be used. Should the counselor ask the clinic for partial assistance, or should he ask the clinic to assume full responsibility? The clinic was reluctant to provide partial services; they preferred to take complete charge. Because of the excellent rapport between the counselor and Otto, and because he believed that if his theories were correct he could be effective with Otto, the counselor felt that greater and more immediate help could be provided if the clinic only supplied partial services.

Dolores was a sophomore in high school and had serious under-achievement problems. The counselor was suspicious of her aptitude and standardized achievement test scores. Dolores lived in a home plagued by parents who were aggressively hostile to each other, and who used Dolores as a kind of psychological battering ram. The counselor felt that he could offer some help to the girl within the school framework. First, however, he felt it necessary to obtain additional test data, and so requested the help of a school psychometrist. His specific request was for the results of three particular tests. The psychometrist, however, provided a relatively complete case study on Dolores. The psychometrist felt that test data alone were worse than no data at all, and consequently, with the best of intentions, completed a case study. An incidental result of the case work, however, was to further upset the parents and Dolores to the point where counselor-student rapport was permanently destroyed.

As these illustrations suggest, it is easy in the process of referring students to lose sight of the students' needs and spend time and energy arguing over professional rights and petty jealousies. Perhaps by keeping the needs of the students paramount, the counselor and referral agency personnel can work out optimal understandings as to who is to provide which services. Using the needs of students as a reference point should facilitate mutual understanding of school and agency philosophies and policies, even if mutual acceptance cannot be achieved. In addition, it should provide a basis for changing philosophies and policies so that they can better serve the needs of students.

The second factor in determining the nature of a particular referral should be the extent to which others besides the student, the counselor, and agency personnel are to be involved in the referral process. The two most obvious categories of "others" are parents and school personnel. Referrals can be made so as to involve only the student, counselor, and referral personnel, or so as to involve progressively several other groups of people in varying degrees.

Again, the well-being of the counselee should be the primary criterion in the determination. If, for example, involving parents in a referral action can benefit the student, then they should be actively involved. If, on the other hand, particular parents manifest attitudes and more overt behavior which suggest that involving them in a referral process would actually inhibit the favorable outcome of the referral on the student, then the counselor should attempt to limit their involvement to a minimum. If this statement appears to hedge, it reflects the limitations on the schools' responsibility for students. In many situations, parents must necessarily be involved in referral action because of parents' basic responsibility for their children, and the resultant necessity for schools to secure parents' approval of atypical or nonroutine practices. It may help to keep in mind that there is a difference between informing parents or securing their approval, and actively involving them. It is not being suggested here that parents be deceived, or even left uninformed, but that the counselor attempt to involve them in referral processes only in terms of the contributions they can make towards benefiting their child.

The involvement of teachers and administrators in referral actions presents a somewhat different problem. Administrators are of course personally responsible for any actions in which students are involved by school personnel. While this responsibility is a tremendous one, it differs in at least two significant aspects from the responsibility of parents for children. First, the lines of responsibility within the school, for example, from a principal to a counselor, can be established and agreed upon, thus minimizing ambiguity as to what the counselor is allowed to do, what student confidences he can expect to maintain, and similar points. Thus, with adequate preparation, the counselor should be in a position to know how far he must involve administrators in referrals before the referral decision is made, and without consulting administrators in each case.

Second, active involvement of administrators in a referral action is less likely in general to be beneficially pertinent. That is, in most cases the administrator has not been involved in the counseling process, and although he gives administrative support for the counselor, he is not in a position to make a unique contribution. Involving him in the referral simply necessitates burdening him with the details of the case. Again, there is a distinction to be made between informing and active involvement.

The involvement of teachers in the referral is somewhat different from involving administrators and very different from involving parents. Obviously, teachers are not responsible for a total school program, as administrators are. Teachers are often in a position to provide information and suggestions pertinent to a particular referral case. They work with the student daily and offer great potential for implementing or reinforcing the findings and efforts of a referral source. Thus the discriminating and perceptive counselor should be able to benefit a counselee by selectively involving teachers in what might be termed as pre- and post-referral situations.

Under the third heading, the implementation of referrals, several factors may be considered. First, it is important that both the counselor and the referral agency understand why a student has been referred and the respective roles to be played by the two parties. What is expected, who has been involved, and what those involved have been told about the agency need to be understood on both sides. If the agency provides only a diagnostic service, and cannot offer immediate therapeutic assistance, all those involved should know it. If the school anticipates suspending or expelling a student being referred, the agency should be informed. Without a mutually acceptable understanding, both the agency and the counselor are likely to waste much time and effort, and more important, instill or reinforce a feeling of futility in the student and his parents.

A second factor which needs attention at the time of referral is the kind and extent of information to be given to the referral agency by the school. Certainly one general guide line which can be followed in nearly all referral cases is that a student's confidence should not be violated without the permission of the student. It is simply not ethical to obtain information under the promise that it will be held in confidence and then communicate the information to others against the counselee's will, even though such communication appears to be in his best interest. This is not the nature of counseling.

Given the counselee's permission to communicate information, it is then up to the counselor to determine the kind and extent of information to be passed on. A second guide line would be to communicate information on a selective basis. That is, the counselor should provide only that information which is relevant to the objectives of the referral action. The extent to which particular kinds of information should be communicated is a function of the psychological sophistication of the referral agency. Consider the following illustrations.

Mary was a high-ability, high-achieving senior student, with college aspirations. Her home was broken, and her parents could not or would not finance a college education. She could partially finance the education with a part time job, but would need additional funds. A local Kiwanis club had a fund for needy students, but required a formal application and interview before considering a case. Mary's counselor asked the club for referral assistance and was in turn requested to supply certain information. Part of the data form and the counselor's responses are reproduced below.

*Intelligence:* Adequate for educational aspirations.

*Achievement:* Current achievement indicates high probability of making better than average marks in college.

*Personality:* Personable, considerate of others, strong personal drive and initiative, potential leadership ability.

Concerned about learning a profession, needs and responds well to encouragement about her accomplishments.

*Family Circumstances:* No financial assistance available for college.

No apparent interest in Mary's attending college. Other family circumstances such that chance of Mary's finishing local college if she continued to live at home very poor. No personal or family problems anticipated in leaving home for college.

Sue was a similar case, except that her counselor believed that financial assistance alone would not provide an adequate solution to the problem. Sue's parents were not merely uninterested in her attending college, but were actually antagonistic towards the idea and stated that she could not attend, regardless of how much financial assistance she received from outside sources. Neither parent had achieved more than an eighth-grade education. The counselor learned from Sue that a divorce was imminent. After a conference with Sue's mother, the counselor suspected that Sue's college aspirations were operating as a serious threat to the parents' feelings of adequacy about themselves and their marriage. The counselor, besides helping Sue to obtain financial assistance, secured her permission to seek the referral assistance of a local Family Service Agency. The agency agreed to help Sue overcome her parents' resistence. They asked the counselor for information similar to that in the case of Mary. The counselor's responses are reproduced below.

*Intelligence:* Kuhlman-Anderson IQ Grade 11 = 1 2 3 (Sr. High School Test)

*Achievement:* G.P.A. (5 semesters) 3.51 (A = 4) Iowa Test of Educational Development Composite Scores (Grade 12; form X3S) 97 percentile

*Personality:*  Personable, considerate of others. Some reluctance to participate as much as she wants in social activities because of
uncertainty about her family status—often makes her
overly cautious in assuming leadership roles. Removal
from home situation would probably help decrease over-
cautiousness. Has a strong personal drive to succeed, but
often inhibits this with her reluctance to have faith in
her associates. In general, very favorably perceived by
others.

*Family*
*Circumstances:*  Parents opposed to college plans. Parents dissatisfied with
each other and their marriage, according to mother.
Father feels inadequate. Denies value of education, and
particularly resents education for women. Mother reports
unhappiness for other reasons, but would discontinue resistance to college plans if father would. Mother wants
Sue out of the home—fears that she will continue to
reside in home if she doesn't attend college. I suspect that
father has same feeling but feels guilty about admitting
it. I think that for the particular objective in question, a
couple of sessions with the father would solve the resistance problem.

In the first illustration, the counselor's objective was to assure the
referral source that in his professional judgment Mary was qualified
and deserving of assistance. Information stated in general terms provided the necessary documentation. There was no need for specific and
detailed information. The objectives in the case of Sue, however, were
quite different. A professional agency was being asked to provide counseling for the girl's parents. The agency felt that unless the girl possessed
significantly high academic and personal strength, their brief efforts
with the parents stood a good chance of ultimate failure. The counselor
attempted to support the contention that if the girl could manage to begin college, she had the intellectual and psychological strength to pursue
her educational and vocational plans regardless of her parents' attitudes.
The data and counselor observation transmitted were intended to facilitate a social worker's attempt to change a parent's attitude on at least a
short-term basis.

Closely related to the question of how much information is to be
transmitted to referral sources is the matter of feedback to and from the
counselor and the referral sources. This point has been touched on before. A point frequently raised by competent school counselors is the
problem of getting adequate feedback from referral sources. One can

speculate on the reasons for this. Perhaps, in days past, when the vast majority of school counselors were teachers with little or no professional preparation for counseling, various other professional groups simply lacked confidence in counselors' ability to understand and use feedback information. Perhaps, at best, they felt that the information would merely satisfy a counselor's curiosity and would seldom influence the school's reaction to the student. Perhaps other professional personnel failed to realize the impact of school influences on young people and that their own efforts to help a student were seriously limited when they failed to work with school personnel.

Whatever the reasons, there seems to be a greater interest and willingness on the part of counselors and nonschool agencies to cooperate and to complement each other's efforts to help young people. In view of this, what can the counselor do to encourage more adequate feedback? First, he can, as has been suggested, make careful and considered referrals. That is, after considering the implications of a given referral, he can supply the referral agency with pertinent and unambiguous data. He is then in a favorable position to expect professional cooperation from referral agency personnel. He is then justified in requesting a mutual understanding about what information shall be exchanged. If he can demonstrate his ability to use feedback information and to help referral personnel develop more appropriate kinds of information, he should be providing a basis for increased mutual understanding and respect between various helping professions and agencies. Some might argue that the burden is not entirely with school counselors and other guidance personnel, but rather should be shared by nonschool agencies. This contention, though justifiable, appears to be somewhat beside the point. Counselors will not receive the respect which will lead to more adequate feedback until they themselves initiate efforts to demonstrate their ability to use such information.

A final consideration pertinent to the implementation of a referral is that of developing an understanding with the counselee about the effect the referral will have on the school counselor-counselee relationship. An illustration follows:

Mr. Kerns had been Marvin's school counselor for two years. They had established an excellent counseling relationship, allowing Marvin to feel completely free to include his most personal problems in counseling sessions. During his senior year Marvin needed help with a family problem which the counselor felt could be provided more effectively by a nonschool agency. Marvin agreed to a referral, and thus a third person was actively included in the counseling process. At this point, the relationship between Marvin and Mr. Kerns might have been definitely affected. Marvin could have experienced considerable confusion and anxiety over who was to be told what, and other details. Mr. Kerns also might have experienced resentment if Marvin was reluctant to discuss his counseling with the new person. It is possible, of course, to initiate referrals without any such effect on the established counseling relationship. To insure this, however, the counselor can discuss with the counselee the rules of the game, or the absence of them, regarding a referral. If the counselor expects to discuss the referral proceedings with the counselee, this should be made clear. If the counselee does not want to discuss the referral proceedings with the counselor in future sessions, this should also be stated. The particular decisions in a given case are up to the counselor and the counselee to determine. The decision, however, should be made and understood prior to the referral.

In summary, referrals represent one means of securing additional help for counselees. Referrals are not a panacea in difficult counseling cases. They may or may not be of assistance, depending upon the availability of adequate and competent referral agencies, the school context within which the counselor must operate, the amount of careful consideration given to the referral, and the basic mutual understanding between all involved with which it is implemented.

## PARENT CONFERENCES

The parent-counselor conference procedure operating in an increasing number of secondary schools poses problems that are unique to school counselors, at least in relative frequency. The following discussion is devoted to some of the counseling implications of parent-counselor conferences and is included in this chapter because these conferences represent, in part at least, counseling tasks which transcend the various counseling contexts as described in Chapter 1.

It may be helpful at the outset to distinguish the different objectives for which parent conferences are held. These are not mutually exclusive. Several of them can be objectives for a particular parent conference with perfect consistency. They are as follows:

1. Provide achievement and aptitude data.
2. Make educational plans.

3. Help parents understand their children's abilities and potentials.
4. Help parents understand and accept their children and their environmental variables, including their parents.
5. Help parents whose children have specific behavior problems.

This list could be expanded but is sufficient for present purposes.

If the only purpose of a parent conference is to provide and explain test results, grades, and similar matters, there is relatively little danger of destroying an established counseling relationship. The parent can become upset and defensive about test results (his assertions about his offspring can be disconfirmed) and he could proceed to destroy his child's confidence in the counselor. But, an interpretation of test results can be accomplished in such a way as to minimize the chances of such an event. However, by minimizing the parents' opportunity to react affectively to an appraisal of their child, the counselor considerably reduces the potential value of the conference. A mere repeating of appraisal data couched in terms designed to make them palatable to parents first, and meaningful and accurate second, is hardly counseling, and may be dishonest.

Somewhat the same thing is true of parent-counselor conferences which are held to make educational plans. Regardless of whether or not the student is included in these conferences, they can be conducted in ways to make them primarily pleasant and acceptable to the parents. The counselor advises an educational program (or sells one) to the parents. A primary consideration is that the parents go home happy. It is not news that many administrators are prone to worry a great deal over public relations. Raising doubts in the minds of parents as to the possibility of their child's being a lawyer or a physicist, or taking advanced social studies or senior mathematics may not always result in good public relations. Thus, if the primary objective of educational planning conferences with parents is good public relations, counseling need not be involved. If the objective, however, is to involve the parents in serious consideration of their child's educational future, and one anticipates that in the process some parents will be disturbed and need help in understanding and accepting certain facts and ideas, then there are counseling implications.

The reasons for listing the third objective separately (that of helping parents understand their children's abilities and potential), rather than assuming it to be included in the first and second objectives, should now be clear. One can, it is contended, fulfill the first two aims without involving counseling implications. In order to achieve this objective, the counselor must open up with the parent, to some extent at least, an area which he and the student have discussed in counseling. Not just test data, but the student's feelings, attitudes, aspirations, and assertions, as well as those of the parents, must be included as part of the content of the conference.

Similarly, when an objective of a parent-counselor conference is that of helping parents understand their child's particular environmental variables, including the parents themselves, the choice between including or excluding counseling implications does not exist. For different reasons, the same thing is true of conferences held to help parents whose children have specific behavior problems.

Now, are there any general considerations to help the counselor hold effective conferences with parents, and at the same time maintain, and even improve, the counseling relationship with the student? The following discussion may provide some helpful suggestions.

Almost everyone could agree that one basic objective of nearly all parent-counselor conferences it to help parents understand their youngsters better. Certainly, as suggested above, there are many specific objectives which are pertinent to specific conferences and foreign to others. That is, specific objectives may have to do with achievement, potential achievement, educational and vocational plans, current adjustment problems, and similar matters. Basically, however, all of these specific objectives contribute in some way to parents' better understanding of their children.

If we accept this concept, it then follows that the frame of reference suggested in Chapter 2 for secondary school counseling can be employed in parent-counselor conferences. It is not the only frame of reference available, obviously. Given this basic objective, however, the frame of reference can be helpful in regard to parent conferences. To be more specific, the counselor, as he begins a conference with parents, asks himself, "How can the information I have about the child of these parents be used to best help them understand and accept the child?" If he thinks in terms of interference theory, the logical question that follows will be, "What are the major or basic assertions they have about their child?" He will then need to ask questions and provide leads so as to secure an answer to this question. The process will probably involve acceptance, clarification, dealing with hostility, and asking the parents what they mean, how do they know, and similar questions.

As a clear picture of assertions develops, the counselor will begin to see ways in which his knowledge of the child can best be used. Perhaps the parents' assertions are not consistent with a more objective appraisal of the child. This being the case, test data, grades, teacher evaluation, and so on would be used in an attempt to change assertions. Perhaps their assertions are vague. For example, parents who have never given much thought to the academic potential of their very bright child may be helped to develop assertions about his brightness. These will, in turn, facilitate educational and vocational planning that the student has been doing with his counselor.

The process, as suggested, may involve helping the parents resolve conflicts and tension by helping them to understand ways in which assertions are being disconfirmed. For example, the parents who perceive their teen-age daughter as a popular, personable, glamorous, cute coed—but one who seems never to be invited to dances and parties—probably are not in need of more information. They are more apt to need assistance in understanding, accepting, and dealing with their own feelings about the facts. With such assistance, they may be able to replace redundant behavior with more appropriate methods of attempting to help their daughter. For instance, they may be able to curb their unsuccessful efforts to arrange dates for their daughter by which they have impressed her with her various inadequacies (in their perception), and instead offer her the support and understanding that she needs. They may, as a beginning, be guided to distinguish assertions and disconfirmations about themselves from those about their child.

To put it very simply, parent-counselor conferences can be viewed as counseling sessions. This, of course, assumes that competent counselors are involved, that sufficient time is allowed, and that the parents' understanding of the child is the one basic objective of the conference, and that all other objectives are secondary to that one. Seeing parent-counselor conferences in this perspective, and employing the interference theory frame of reference, permits the counselor to relate to the parent in a professional and effective manner. By making the parents the center of the conference (in what might be called parent-centered counseling), the counselor does not put himself in the position of needing to disclose student confidences, of giving advice, of stating opinions, or of becoming entwined in meaningless praise of the child. He also has constructive means of using information which may be disconfirming. The parents' feelings about their children's characteristics, rather than the children's characteristics in themselves, become the concern of the parent-counselor conference.

## Suggested References

*Using Environmental Information in Counseling*

Roe, Anne, "The Implications of Occupational Psychology," in *The Psychology of Occupations,* Wiley, 1956, chap. 24.

Tolbert, E. L., "Using Occupational, Educational, and Social Information in Counseling," in *Introduction to Counseling,* McGraw-Hill, 1959, chap. 10.

Tyler, Leona E., "The Counselor's Use of Occupational Information," in *The Work of the Counselor,* Appleton-Century-Crofts, 1953, chap. VI.

*Test Interpretation*

Bennett, George K., Harold G. Seashore, and Alexander G. Wesman, *Counseling from Profiles,* The Psychological Corporation, 1951.

Bordin, Edward S., "Test Selection and Interpretation" and "Illustrations and Problems," in *Psychological Counseling,* Appleton-Century-Crofts, 1955, chaps. 11, 12.

Tyler, Leona E., "Integrating Tests with the Counseling Process," in *The Work of the Counselor,* Appleton-Century-Crofts, 1953, chap. VI.

*Referrals*

Mortenson, Donald G., and Allen M. Schmuller, "Referral Resources," in *Guidance in Today's Schools,* Wiley, 1959, chap. 14.

........................................................................

# CHAPTER 7

# Contributions of Noncounseling Guidance Procedures to Counseling

Counseling in secondary schools is not intended to be a service that is complete in itself. Although, in the perspective of this book, counseling is the primary function of a school guidance program, there are a number of noncounseling guidance procedures for which counselors must assume varying degrees of responsibility. The following list could be more detailed, but it encompasses the guidance activities for which counselors logically could be expected to have some direct responsibility.

1. Student appraisal procedures.
2. Student class scheduling.
3. Group guidance procedures.
4. Working with nonschool agencies.
5. Assisting staff members.
6. Student placement services.
7. Maintaining environmental information.
8. Local research and guidance development.

Each of these aspects of school guidance has specific objectives as well as the common objective of facilitating counseling. The purpose of this chapter is to suggest how the various noncounseling aspects of guidance may be perceived so as to facilitate this common objective. The specific objectives and procedures of each of the noncounseling guidance areas are not within the scope of this book.

Noncounseling guidance procedures can facilitate both directly and indirectly the counselor's efforts to help students within counseling itself. One can expect effective work in these areas to have a direct influence on counseling. It is also important to realize that effective work in these areas can influence the attitudes and procedures of administrative and teaching personnel so as to facilitate counseling efforts indirectly. The discussion that follows is presented in terms of this classification, arbitrary as it may be in certain respects. This is done primarily to emphasize that in secondary schools, at least, a factor important to successful counseling is the attitude of faculty members toward a guidance program.

## DIRECT FACILITATION OF COUNSELING

The guidance procedures listed above can have several kinds of direct influence on students that are important to counseling. These procedures function as (1) orientation of students towards reasonable expectations regarding counseling procedures, (2) means by which decisions evolving from counseling can be implemented, (3) sources of help in satisfying needs identified during counseling, (4) sources of information important for counselee self-understanding.

This idea will be developed through brief consideration of each of the guidance aspects listed according to the four kinds of influences.

Table 2 summarizes the relationship discussed in the following paragraphs, and may help to clarify the discussion. In the table the single and double x's indicate the degree of importance of the relationship. The following discussion is intended to provide a more definitive description of the nature of these relationships.

### Student Appraisal Procedures

As used here, the term *student appraisal procedures* refers to all systematic attempts to identify individual differences among students. Appraisal procedures can be classified as group or individual, test or nontest, instructional or guidance, and so on, but functionally, all appraisal data can be of direct assistance to counselees.

Table 2 suggests that the greatest direct influence appraisal data can have on counseling is as sources of information in assisting students to gain accurate self-understanding. To this end, appraisal data should be available in terms which are meaningful to students. Essentially, this means that the counselor ought to be in a position to present appraisal

TABLE 2. Relative Importance of Noncounseling Guidance Procedures as Direct Influences on Counseling[a]

| Procedures | Types of Direct Influence | | | |
| --- | --- | --- | --- | --- |
| | Orientation of Students Towards Reasonable Expectations of Counseling | Means of Implementing Decision Made During Counseling | Sources of Help in Satisfying Needs Identified During Counseling | Source of Information Important for Self-understanding |
| Student appraisal procedures | x | | x | xx |
| Student class scheduling | x | xx | xx | |
| Group guidance procedures | xx | | xx | x |
| Working with nonschool agencies | | x | xx | x |
| Assisting staff members | x | xx | xx | x |
| Student placement services | | xx | x | |
| Maintaining environmental information | | x | xx | x |
| Local research and development | | x | xx | x |

[a] Not based on actual data.

data in descriptive (narrative) and predictive terminology. For example, it is much more meaningful for a student to know that of students who have had grade point averages similar to his, and who attended the college in which he anticipates enrolling, 45 percent make grade point averages of C or below, rather than to be told that the correlation between high school G.P.A. and freshman grades in that college is .55. Similarly, learning that he measures high in outdoor and mechanical interests provides much less potential for self-understanding than does knowing his measured interests are quite similar to those of people in certain occupations and quite unlike those of people in certain other occupations. To know the percentile equivalents of one's Differential Aptitude Test scores is not as meaningful to the student as to know the various typical levels of performances achieved by those having similar Differential Aptitude Test performances.

To the same end, appraisal data need to be of sufficient scope to facilitate the testing of numerous kinds of assertions by the student. In some instances, this does not mean that the student will have actual data, but rather, that the counselor needs information (such as an autobiography) to guide him in asking questions which will help the student in his efforts toward self-understanding.

In addition to having data pertinent to various areas of counselee concern, the counselor should secure appraisal information covering the various levels of student ability. For example, student rating scales completed by teachers should not be limited to measurement of characteristics important to college success. Just as important are teacher ratings of terminal students according to nonacademic variables related to job success. Similarly, predictive data of standardized test results should be available for terminal as well as college preparatory students.

Student appraisal procedures can also have a direct influence in helping students meet needs identified during counseling. As counseling progresses and students begin to verbalize various assertions, they frequently request information about themselves so that assertions can be confirmed. As this happens, counselors may want to initiate additional appraisal, or more ideally, they may be able to draw upon data already collected in the school's appraisal program. While counselors cannot anticipate all of the various needs for self-information that counselees will identify, attention to insuring adequate scope in the appraisal program will pay off in counseling assistance to students. Somehow many school people have assumed that adequate use of test results means reporting or interpreting each score he has obtained to each student in school. Such an assumption neglects one of the main justifications for group appraisal procedures, that is, economy. The cost of giving and scoring a single individual intelligence test to a high school sophomore, for example, is nearly as much as that of administering a group test to thirty students. There are many important uses for both individual and group tests. If one only considers, however, their function in helping students obtain better self-understanding, then the economy criterion has been met if only five or six group scores are actually used. The point was made earlier that test results should be used in counseling only when the student needs the information. Thus, systematically, or as it may be, compulsively interpreting all of a student's test results to him is rather misguided economy. By the same reasoning, having the information available in anticipation of individual needs that will arise makes good sense economically.

Finally, appraisal procedures can have direct influence on orienting students as to what they can reasonably expect in counseling. For many students, the activity of taking various kinds of tests and inventories, writing autobiographies, and completing sociometric devices will suggest and redefine problems and questions in a context more closely akin to the counseling situation. By giving some particular thought to the incidental reaction of students to appraisal procedures, and by providing appropriate preparation for each procedure applied, the counselor can help students focus on the total appraisal-counseling process. In such preparation, the counselor is saying to students, "These are some of the kinds of things that you can discuss in counseling—these facts, as well as your feelings about the facts."

## Student Class Scheduling

From the point of view of many school administrators, counseling and scheduling are nearly synonymous terms. From the perspective of this book, scheduling, that is, the selection of a particular program of courses for a semester or a year, is not counseling, but primarily a means by which students implement decisions that they have made during or after counseling. In larger schools, the actual scheduling can be done by data processing machines to the benefit of school personnel and without any disadvantage to students. Scheduling is simply the mechanics of making certain kinds of decisions operative. This is not to suggest that scheduling is unimportant to secondary school counseling. Indeed, the opposite is true. Without effective scheduling procedures, a good part of educational counseling becomes meaningless. What point is there in helping students make decisions, unless they can become operative? Similarly, is there any justification in helping students identify needs which can be satisfied within the course offerings of a school if scheduling procedures are so rigid as to seriously inhibit attempts at satisfaction?

It is obvious to anyone who has taught in high school that scheduling, by its very nature, cannot help but have a direct influence on counseling efforts. Thus, counselors have a responsibility to see that the influence will encourage, rather than inhibit, student decisions and the satisfaction of needs. In some schools, administrative policies and procedures place definite limitations on the counselor's efforts in this area. In others, counselors have major administrative responsibilities. Some of these responsibilities are not our concern here. We are more interested in those which nearly all counselors can accept.

Paramount among them is that the counselor understand scheduling limitations himself, and then communicate these to his counselees as information which they need in order to make appropriate and reliable program decisions. If, for example, a counselee's test scores preclude his taking a particular course, he needs to know this. This is a fact of real importance, and incidentally, one which the counselor need not be embarrassed to relate. Here, too, is an illustration of the difference between scheduling as synonymous with counseling and scheduling as a means of implementing decisions. In the former situation, a fact is simply stated, and often defended, by the advisor. In the latter situation, the student has an opportunity to discuss his feelings about the fact. He can explore its possible implications for his future, and how it relates to assertions making up his current self-understandings.

A second important responsibility that nearly all counselors can assume is that of defining for the student the extent of his responsibility in making his own educational plans. If, for example, the school policy is such that the students' programs are in large part determined by test data, and the counselor's task is one of selling or coercing, or just plain signing students up for the courses, then it is important to future counseling efforts that the student not be under the initial illusion that this is counseling. The sophomore, for example, who has his first counseling experience in high school under the conditions just described, will leave the interview with a perspective on counseling which probably will not favorably influence his expectations of future counseling. Under such circumstances, the course selection procedure should be explained to students. Again, should the student want to discuss his feelings about what others have planned and selected for him, understanding that the counselor cannot revise the decision, then counseling is certainly appropriate.

## Group Guidance

The phrase *group guidance* includes such a variety of activities as to render it almost meaningless by itself. Many group procedures in guidance are essentially applications of traditional classroom activities (e.g., vocational study units and occupational and career lectures), while at the other extreme some group guidance procedures are essentially therapeutic efforts (e.g., multiple counseling and sociodrama). If a limitation were to be placed on the definition of group guidance employed here, it would be that of excluding or placing less emphasis on those procedures at the therapeutic end of the continuum. Such a limitation is defensible within the present secondary school context, at least in regard to the probable frequency with which the various group guidance procedures are used.

In Table 2, the two most important types of direct influence on counseling ascribed to group guidance procedures are orientation of students toward counseling and sources of help in satisfying needs identified during counseling. Of the two, the former is probably more frequently recognized on an operational level by school counselors. Frequently, for example, back-to-school orientation days give specific attention to the counseling services available to students, usually in descriptive form. In one school a short "demonstration interview" is presented for the new students as part of their orientation. Various kinds of counselor-sponsored group guidance meetings, such as Armed Forces Day and Career Day, end with the suggestion that students discuss what they have learned with their counselors. Classroom group guidance procedures often give explicit and implied counseling orientation to students. Classroom guidance procedures also provide opportunities for helping students anticipate the kinds of help they might obtain from counseling.

The second kind of influence, that of a source of help in satisfying needs identified during counseling, is probably given systematic attention less frequently. It has, however, as much or more potential value as the orientation influence of group procedures. At least two means of implementation are being used in schools. Counselors refer students to various existing group procedures as needs are identified. Also, the counselor can actually initiate group procedures according to the common needs that he identifies among his counselees. An illustration of the first suggestion might be a student with particular questions about an occupational field, or perhaps a need to have some kind of identification with a professional person in a field. If a speaker is scheduled to appear at a special program, or at a class in which the student is not enrolled, the counselor can make the opportunity known to the student, and possibly even assist him in making arrangements to attend, if this should be a problem.

The second suggestion is somewhat more difficult to implement, but is a part of some school guidance programs. For example, one junior high school counselor in a school with students of generally low socio-economic background, primarily from minority groups, forms several clubs each school year. The clubs are varied in objectives and membership. One such club consisted of six high-ability, severely underachieving boys, another consisted of seven boys who from all available evidence were on the borderline of serious delinquent behavior. A third group consisted of six boys, two each from the three racial groups represented in the school, all of whom had considerable leadership potential, but were unable to begin experiencing leadership responsibility. As potential members are identified in counseling, opportunity to join the groups is extended. Other kinds of group procedures of a less therapeutic nature also can be initiated according to the needs identified in counseling, assuming adequate personnel are available. Study groups for all levels of students, vocational clubs, and special lectures for students and parents are examples of these. While the counselor can anticipate many student needs, and cooperate with other faculty members in establishing group procedures to help meet these, other needs are common to only a few students at a given time. With the implied motivation potential, perhaps activities initiated on this basis have the greatest value of all group procedures in guidance.

The direct influence of group guidance procedures on counseling in terms of sources of information important for counselee self-understanding has been treated, at least by implication and suggestion, in the several paragraphs above. To put the matter very briefly, one can employ group procedures to help students achieve more accurate self-understandings. While there are more accurate, reliable, and objective sources of factual information about one's environment than the typical group guidance procedure, this frequently entails advantages. It may serve as a means of personal identification with status figures, it may allow dramatization, or help in other ways important to individual students at particular times.

## Working with Nonschool Agencies

Most of what needs to be said here about the importance of the direct influence of nonschool agencies on counseling has been discussed in Chapter 6. Essentially, these agencies can be perceived by counselors as referral agencies, offering a service or funds which will help students satisfy needs or implement decisions, or in some instances, provide needed information. Because of their particular objectives, facilities, and personnel, these agencies are often able to provide assistance not available within the school system, or at least to supplement the school's efforts to help students with special problems. Referral sources can assist the more typical students. Their greatest importance to the counselor, however, is in the help they can offer to the relatively atypical students, whom, because he must attempt to serve all students, the counselor frequently has to neglect.

## Working with Staff Members

There seem to be indications today of a movement to view counselors primarily as guidance consultants to teachers and administrators, rather than as personnel with special competencies which are most effectively used in counseling with students. The fear of counseling specialists in certain quarters has been with us for some time, and will probably continue to exist for many years to come. This question in itself is not the concern of this section, but is pertinent to a discussion of how the counselor can work with other faculty members so as to facilitate his counseling efforts. The position taken here is that counselors certainly can and need to provide consultant services to teachers, as long as these services are provided in addition to, rather than in place of, a primary emphasis on counseling with students. Assuming then that counselors view their main function as counseling, and that they also feel an important responsibility to help teachers and administrators to understand and assist students with problems, what are some ways in which they can provide the latter services so as to facilitate their counseling efforts?

Table 2 emphasizes the direct importance of this noncounseling responsibility to counseling in showing a relationship between the area and all four categories of facilitation. Basic to the whole question, of course, are the attitudes of faculty members towards counselors and guidance activities of counselors. This topic will be discussed in a later section of this chapter. Referring to Table 2 again, however, in relation to the direct influence of the area on counseling, note that its two most important influences indicated are as means of implementing decisions made during counseling, and as sources of help in satisfying needs identified during counseling. It has been stated earlier that one of the most frequent kinds of decisions students make in connection with counseling is that of selecting the courses that will best contribute to implementing educational and vocational decisions. Many times these are difficult decisions. They are seldom made without ambivalence, misgiving, and great uncertainty as to their appropriateness. While the counselor can be expected to have little influence on the content of a course and the methods a teacher employs, he can often cooperate with teachers in noncontent areas. For example, if motivation is a real problem, cooperation between counselor and teacher may result in teacher efforts to motivate the student which are more appropriate to his particular needs and attitudes than would be possible without the cooperation of the counselor. Likewise, cooperation between teacher and counselor may help the teacher, and the counselor as well, to provide psychologically meaningful support to the student at particularly appropriate times. As a matter of fact, if the counselor is successful in his attempts to help the teacher with an understanding of several students, it is quite possible that actual changes in course content may be effected so as to help a student implement a particularly difficult and important decision.

Working with teachers and faculty towards the end of providing sources of help for satisfying needs identified during counseling can result in other changes. As has been stated in almost every textbook on teaching methods, teachers have greater opportunity than any other school personnel to work with children in a greater variety of ways. Students identify, respect, fear, idolize, and emulate their teachers. They also seek advice from them, aim hostility at them, and react toward them in a variety of other ways. When counselors identify various needs among students, their working with teachers can help teachers understand these needs. Consequently, teachers may become more accepting of students than would otherwise be the case. Possibly teachers can provide opportunities for students to practice some of the insights gained through counseling.

As Table 2 also suggests, working with staff members can also have a direct influence on counseling in terms of orienting students toward counseling, and as sources of information important for counselee self-understanding. The latter influence has been discussed above in another context, and has to do primarily with counselors' helping teachers work in terms of individual needs of specific students. Orientation, in regard to working with teachers, has also been treated within the discussion of group guidance procedures, and need not be given more attention here.

## Student Placement Services

The term *student placement,* as used here, refers to the part of a guidance program designed to help students make a satisfactory transition from high school to whatever they decide to do after leaving school. Essentially, placement is usually made to one of three types of situation: higher education, vocational education, or employment. The responsibility for the placement aspect of guidance is generally assumed by all counselors in a school, but sometimes certain specific placement duties are the responsibility of one counselor, and in some large districts special placement counselors, or even placement departments, assume this function.

Table 2 suggests that the most important direct influence placement has on counseling is as a means of implementing decisions students make during counseling. This is a rather obvious point, and need not be labored here. Several cautions, however, are pertinent. First, counselors need to work consistently to insure that the placement function is oriented to the needs of students rather than to the needs of colleges, schools, and employers. These needs, of course, are not altogether in opposition, and, in fact, often are a function of each other. However, students should be protected from pressures and biases of recruitment if placement services are to be of maximum service to counseling with students. To achieve this, counselors must be aware of the nature and needs of various placement sources, and must have confidence in the type of contacts that the personnel from these sources have with students. In addition, specific attention should be devoted to providing the broadest possible scope of placement possibilities. Limited placement contacts place unnecessary restrictions on the vocational and educational horizons of individual students. In order to facilitate counseling, the placement service needs to develop new placement sources, as well as provide contacts with those already identified.

A third caution deserving attention is that of insuring against the making of placement decisions for the student by others, either overtly or through more subtle methods, such as biased, inadequate or invalid presentations, or undue pressures. Probably because of the importance of placement decisions in a student's life, adults are especially anxious to provide advice to the extent of virtually making the decision for the student. Thus, counselors need to be especially careful to provide counselees with opportunities to work out their own placement decisions.

Finally, an important direct influence of placement on counseling is as a source of help in satisfying needs identified in counseling. Placement can of course satisfy very important material needs by providing sources of income for students while they are still in school. In addition, placement also can help students by satisfying work experience needs of both the job knowledge and self-knowledge categories. Adequate placement services, when readily available to a counselor, can often serve as avenues to experiential supports for those things which the student is experiencing in counseling.

## Environmental Information

Information on occupations, schools, colleges, and financial aid to students has traditionally been an important aspect of guidance in secondary schools. The most important direct influence this information has on counseling is as a source of help for satisfying needs identified during counseling, primarily needs for information. Again, the manner in which this influence operates is rather obvious. Many excellent discussions of the various uses and implications of environmental information are available. A point common to most of these discussions and deserving of emphasis here is that the intelligent use of environmental information in counseling is a much more complex procedure than one would believe in observing some counselors. The difficulties of selective use of environmental information, and the variation in its accessibility to students, its readability, and its validity, require that counselors give it more than incidental attention. Inadequate information, or ineffective use of appropriate information, can easily reduce the value of the time and effort spent in counseling.

To a lesser extent, environmental information has a direct influence on counseling as a means of implementing decisions made in counseling and as a source of information important for counselee self-understanding. The operation of the first influence is evident. A student makes a decision and then often needs to have detailed information to help him implement his plan. The second influence, on counselee self-understanding, is somewhat nebulous. However, used in conjunction with appraisal data, environmental information can offer a means of testing assertions about oneself. Knowing something about his scholastic aptitude and interests, for example, a student can test to some extent the appropriateness of his vocational plans by studying vocational booklets, college programs, and similar material.

## Local Research and Development

The research and development area encompasses a total guidance program, and is treated in a separate chapter. A discussion of its direct influence on counseling is deferred to that chapter.

## INDIRECT INFLUENCE ON COUNSELING

The suggestion was made in the introduction to this chapter that in addition to having direct influence on counseling, the noncounseling aspects of a guidance program also can have indirect influence by affecting attitudes of staff members towards guidance. The purpose of the following paragraphs is to expand this statement. For lack of a better term, this area might be called *internal public relations,* in the broadest meaning of the phrase.

It probably goes without saying that there is greater opportunity for faculty members to observe the operation and influence of noncounseling guidance procedures than of counseling itself. Essentially, this is because of the confidential nature of counseling. Counseling consists of a personal relationship between the counselor and the student. No one else is invited to participate in the interview, and as a matter of fact, by definition no one else is even allowed to participate directly. What is true of observing the operation of counseling is almost equally true of observing behavior changes resulting from counseling. These are most often changes in attitudes, feelings, and understandings which many times are not manifested in overt behavior changes uncontaminated by other influences.

On the other hand, the opportunities for faculty members to observe the operation and results of noncounseling guidance procedures are many. Here there is not the confidentiality nor the private relationship of counseling, and teachers themselves are frequently involved in varying degrees in these procedures. Teachers can ask, "What have you got?" and "What do you do?" about noncounseling procedures with much more success than they can about counseling. They can easily see the tests and use the results, read placement reports, be part of a group guidance activity, or observe other procedures.

What are some specific ways in which teachers' perceptions of noncounseling guidance procedure indirectly influence counseling? Perhaps discussion of four ways will suggest other ideas to the reader.

A very obvious indirect influence is the evaluation of counselors and counseling that teachers and administrators communicate to students. The author and certainly many of his readers have heard teachers openly degrade various aspects of a school guidance program, including counseling, to students. There is little question that this influences the student's expectation of what counseling has to offer. Many times, by demonstrating the worth of noncounseling procedures to a teacher and then reinforcing his association of counseling with these procedures, a negative attitude can be tempered. If nothing else, the counselor should work towards raising enough doubt in the mind of the teacher of the validity of his evaluation of counseling as to result in his using greater discretion in influencing students.

Many teachers feel that they have a responsibility to contribute to guidance and that they have definite contributions to make to a guidance program. They are certainly justified in their desire to contribute. Of particular pertinence here is the consideration that unless they are included in the guidance program and given a chance to contribute, they will probably resent and resist many of the counselors' efforts. No indirect influence can affect counseling efforts with students more strongly than faculty members who are offering active resistance to the heart of the guidance program. Counselors who refuse to involve teachers desiring to take part in aspects of a guidance program would probably benefit from a little counseling themselves. Obviously, the involvement of faculty members very often demands considerable skill and patience, but the dividends to counseling alone represent an excellent return.

A third indirect influence that teachers' perceptions of a guidance program can have on counseling lies in the student referrals made to counselors. Teachers who view *counseling* as a progressive education term for discipline generally place limitations on counseling simply by the method, or lack of method, by which they refer a student. Too often students are told, "One more stunt like that and I'll march you right down to the counselor." Similarly, counselors hear such statements from teachers as "I'm fed up to the ears with him—you take him during my class today and if you can straighten him out, I'll take him back tomorrow; otherwise, don't send him back to my class." To put it mildly, students can be exasperating at times, and very likely can benefit temporarily from disciplinary methods. However, teachers are likely to make more appropriate referrals if they understand some aspects of the guidance program which they can associate with counseling. At least, there will be a greater probability of their taking time to talk with a counselor about a student before the "last straw" has been laid on the pile.

Finally, it may be helpful to suggest some things the counselor can do for teachers to facilitate their perceptions of guidance and thus indirectly influence counseling. There are innumerable kinds of assistance, and the following three examples are not necessarily the most basic. They illustrate one important consideration, however, in that each is a relatively tangible kind of help, of which immediate use can be made. Particularly in the initial stages of a guidance program, it is important to demonstrate simply and directly that guidance services are helpful.

Normative data about students are available in some form in most schools. However, due to busy schedules, lack of skills, or even lack of awareness of their potential value to instruction, teachers fail to organize and use them to achieve more comprehensive understanding of their classes. Without taking up a prohibitive amount of time, counselors can organize such data in ways meaningful and helpful to teachers. Socio-economic normative data for a class are often instructive to teachers. Parents' education levels, family size, parents' occupations, and so on can give a teacher a new perspective of a class and provide a basis for developing new methods and content for accomplishing teaching objectives.

Recently, there has been a perceptible interest in giving some attention to vocational guidance in subject-matter classes. Teachers are going beyond the teaching of mathematics, chemistry, and government to a consideration of the vocations of mathematician, chemist, and public administrator. Because of their professional preparation, counselors are in an excellent position to suggest and provide appropriate vocational materials to teachers interested in vocational guidance activities.

Helping teachers with placement of terminal students is a third means of promoting teacher understanding of guidance. Most counselors attempt to become and remain familiar with the entry job situation in their geographical area, and thus, whether they have assigned placement responsibility or not, should be able to offer valuable information and assistance in employer contacts to teachers in the business, vocational, and agricultural fields. Teachers often need and appreciate help of this kind. There is little question that their representation of guidance to students will be favorably influenced by such help.

## SUMMARY

This chapter has discussed ways in which noncounseling guidance procedures can contribute to counseling effectiveness. The suggestion has been made that these procedures have a direct influence on counseling, and, through affecting staff members' perceptions of a guidance program, an indirect influence on counseling.

### Suggested References

*Student Appraisal Procedure*

Cronbach, Lee J., *Essentials of Psychological Testing*, 2nd ed., Harper, 1960.
Froehlich, Clifford P., and Kenneth B. Hoyt, *Guidance Testing*, Science Research Associates, 1959.
Tyler, Leona E., "The Use of Tests: Application of Mental Testing Principles to the Counselor's Work," in *The Work of the Counselor*, Appleton-Century-Crofts, 1953, chap. V.

*Group Guidance Procedures*

Froehlich, Clifford, "The Service of Orientation" and "Group Methods in the Information Service," in *Guidance Services in Schools*, McGraw-Hill, 1958, chaps. 6, 7.
McDaniel, Henry B., with G. A. Shaftel, "Group Activities in Guidance," in *Guidance in the Modern School*, Dryden, 1956, chap. 15.
Mortenson, Donald G., and Allen M. Schmuller, "Guidance in Groups," in *Guidance in Today's Schools*, Wiley, 1959, chap. 10.

*Assisting Staff Members*

Froehlich, Clifford, "Teachers and the Guidance Program" and "The Guidance Program and the Curriculum," in *Guidance Services in Schools*, McGraw-Hill, 1958, chaps. 12, 13.

McDaniel, Henry B., with G. A. Shaftel, "Adapting the School to Students' Needs" and "Applying Individual-Inventory Data to the Instruction Program," in *Guidance in the Modern School*, Dryden, 1956, chaps. 13, 14.

Mortenson, Donald G., and Allen M. Schmuller, "Guidance-Oriented Curriculum" and "Guidance in the Learning Process," in *Guidance in Today's Schools*, Wiley, 1959, chaps. 8, 9.

*Placement*

Froehlich, Clifford, "The Service of Placement," in *Guidance Services in Schools*, McGraw-Hill, 1958, chap. 11.

*Maintaining Environmental Information*

Baer, Max F., and Edward C. Roeber, *Occupational Information*, Science Research Associates, 1951.

Tolbert, E. L., "Occupational and Educational Information," in *Introduction to Counseling*, McGraw-Hill, 1959, chap. 9.

....................................................................

# CHAPTER 8

# Counseling Research and Development

As he reads the research literature itself or the various research summaries, the student of counseling cannot help but perceive that the current state of affairs in counseling research is discouraging. There is relatively little research evidence upon which counseling procedures can be based. There are studies concerned with counseling directly, and many more which have implications for counseling. In view, however, of the current and rapidly increasing number of practicing counselors, the field is in dire need of more knowledge about the results of counseling.

Among the various areas of the subject, that counseling which takes place within the context of secondary education probably has received the least research attention of any. This observation is especially appalling if one can accept the idea discussed earlier that counseling in secondary schools is significantly different from counseling in other situations in several important variables.

This chapter is not concerned with summarizing counseling research, a task that has been done admirably by various writers. The references following this chapter include literature surveys and summaries which can provide the reader with a more than basic conception of what has gone on to date. The primary objective here is to encourage school counselors to engage in systematic research and development activities. Admittedly, one must bring more to reasearch than the mere desire to do it. He must also have certain research skills and competencies. It is evident, however, that although some systematic attention in counselor preparation programs is given to research methods and the understanding of research reports, relatively little attention is given to the important role that school counselors themselves need to play in counseling research. After all, where does one find high school counseling, but in high schools? It makes little sense to depend on university personnel to take all of the research responsibilities in the field of counseling. If our school counseling procedures are to be based on research evidence, as well as good ideas, then inevitably, school counselors must take their part. In this chapter the aim of encouraging school counselors to engage in systematic research and development activities will be served through specific attention to counseling criteria, general methodology, and illustrations of suggested school counseling research activities.

## COUNSELING CRITERIA

School counselors who are serious about their profession generally accept the idea that more needs to be known about counseling. Many do not see themselves as researchers, nor feel that research is one of their primary interests, but most genuinely desire to know the results of their efforts and are anxious to make themselves more effective as counselors. Why, then, is not more research being done by school counselors? The author has put this question to many school counselors. Most of the responses can be covered by the following three generalizations:

1. I don't have time to carry on research. What with my other responsibilities, I never seem to complete my counseling and other assigned guidance duties, let alone doing a study.
2. Administrative policy makes it difficult for me to conduct research. My administrators don't want students used as guinea pigs. They say school board members would ask, "If you don't know that counseling works, why are we paying for it?"
3. I don't feel that I have the necessary research skills to do serious experimental work.

Implicit in each generalization is a somewhat stereotyped definition of research: one which probably stems from experiments in physical science. This stereotype is one of the factors that have done most to inhibit counseling research in secondary schools. This is not the appropriate place for a discourse on the philosophy of research in social sciences. It can be stated, however, and illustrated during the remainder of the chapter, that studies in counseling must be based on a relatively broad definition of research. Hence the inclusion of the term *development* in the chapter title. Research is not an esoteric concern of the laboratories of universities and industry. It is any honest and systematic attempt to find out more about what we know less about— a category that would seem to include just about everything. It is an honest attempt in that it is a search for knowledge, rather than a proof of foregone conclusions, and implies recognition of the limitations and qualifications surrounding whatever is discovered. It is systematic in that it requires a statement of what we are about before we begin (our objectives) and an attempt to identify, measure, and record everything within the realm of practical possibility that is pertinent to whatever is being studied.

The reader, recalling that this subsection is entitled Counseling Criteria, may be wondering what all of this has to do with criteria. The crux of the whole school counseling research problem is criteria. The selection of counseling criteria for research is often limited by a somewhat stereotyped conception of research. Ideally, we would like to employ research controls similar to those of the physical sciences. However, strict adherence to such procedures necessitates ignoring many important counseling questions. Perhaps if more attention were given to studying counseling as it is practiced, by whatever procedures are available, more pertinent and specific questions open to rigorous investigation would emerge.

The criteria used in counseling research should conform to the objectives of counseling. Only when this is true can more effective counseling be developed. Most counselors would find it very difficult to examine their efforts in terms of the ultimate objectives of counseling, but certainly meaningful immediate and intermediate objectives of counseling can be kept in mind in research carried on in schools, without encountering many serious methodological or administrative problems.

A further word on development may be helpful. Development can be the improvement of the competencies and procedures of an individual, a local staff, or other organizations up to and including the total professional group. Research at the local level is probably most meaningful when designed as a basis for individual and staff development. Often the problems encountered by an individual counselor or a staff of school counselors are relatively peculiar to a local situation. Placing major emphasis on the solution of local problems is certainly justified. At the same time, it is important to remember that few, if any, problems are totally specific. In other words, honest and systematic attempts to solve local problems often have important implications for workers in other schools and for the profession in general. So-called "local research" has come into disfavor in some quarters, not because of any inherent unworthiness, but rather because of the lack of care with which it has frequently been completed.

Let us finish this section with three basic considerations designed to aid in the selection of appropriate counseling criteria. First, the criteria or objectives should be stated operationally. That is, objectives should be defined in terms of operations which can be observed and measured. For example, a traditional objective of counseling is that of promoting good individual student adjustment or mental hygiene. This seems a reasonable and relatively nonambiguous objective. For certain purposes it probably is, since nearly all of us would admit to some intuitive common understanding of good adjustment or good mental health. However, when the counselor decides to study the extent to which certain of his counselees are achieving this objective, he must inevitably ask himself, "What do I mean by good mental health—how do I measure it?" It is at this point that nonoperational definitions of objectives become useless. Good mental health defined in generalities, as that he has a pleasant personality, he gets along well with others, people like him, and he stays out of trouble, remains ambiguous. These generalities are of little value until they are defined in terms of some observable and measurable operation. That is, pleasant personality needs to be defined in terms of changes on personality measuring instruments, scored reactions of teachers or peers, or similar indications. The statement that people seem to like him needs to be clarified according to sociometric devices, rating scales, and the like; that he stays out of trouble, in terms of frequencies of contacts with certain kinds of authority personnel.

Operational definitions are somewhat arbitrary. After carefully considering the implications of an objective, and the many ways in which it can be manifested, and after examining the instruments and procedures available for measuring it, one must finally decide upon one element, or a combination of several, as defining the objective. There must certainly be an awareness of the limitations of the operational definition employed, but it is unrealistic to refuse to study counseling because perfect operational definitions are not available. In the complex processes of counseling, the choice is not between perfect and imperfect definitions of criteria, but rather between the imperfect and the less imperfect. Take for example, a case in which a staff is systematically counseling with underachievers, defined as those of high ability and low achievement, and has as one of its objectives more appropriate achievement by these students. Several operational definitions of achievement can be used, e.g., grade point average, grades in selected courses, standardized achievement test results, and teachers' observations. Standardized test results are, perhaps, the least contaminated measure, but by that very fact may not include variables, such as classroom conformity, which may be extremely important for future achievement in college. Grade point average may be too general, while selected course grades may exclude certain negative changes in achievement. Further, none of these would be fair to the student who transferred to a more difficult course of study on the basis of counseling, and thus encountered more challenging competition. However, as long as an awareness of these and other limitations is maintained, one is justified in selecting the operational definition which best serves the particular circumstances involved.

Second, the operational definition should be defined so as to be consistent with the practical limitations of the particular school situation, including administrative policy and attitudes towards research and development, financial resources available, flexibility of schedules, and competencies of local counseling personnel. For example, suppose three counselors in a school want to study the influence of counseling with students evidencing serious self-acceptance problems on parental attitudes. One counselor believes that behavior changes in the students would threaten the parents to the extent of disrupting existing home situations, and thus negate any positive influence of the counseling on the students. In the process of selecting an operational definition of counseling, they decide that the criterion measure should ideally involve direct contacts with parents, such as interviews or the administration of an attitude questionnaire. As most readers will recognize, many school systems would simply not tolerate such a project, regardless of how carefully and tactfully it might be conducted. If our three counselors discovered such to be the reaction of their administrators, they would probably need to modify their definition of parental attitudes in terms of these limitations. Whether or not such modifications could be accomplished without destroying the meaningfulness of the resulting operational definition would of course be a decision they would have to make. They might abandon their project and turn to something which could be satisfactorily accomplished within the policies and attitudes of their school system.

Finally, it must be stated that operational definitions of counseling criteria used in the research of school counselors should have practical significance. Traditionally, researchers in counseling and psychotherapy have tended to look with some contempt, or at least patronizingly, upon the use of practical behavior changes as criteria. For example, a boy who had been a source of terror to teachers because of disturbing classroom behavior had several sessions with a counselor and modified his overt behavior so as to become more acceptable to teachers and students. One observer dismissed the changes as insignificant because the boy's former behavior was simply repressed, or inhibited, as a result of counseling. A group of terminal students experienced systematic counseling and had a higher mean income for their first two years of employment after leaving school than a similar group of students not having counseling. Amount of income, however, was criticized as only a superficial measure of vocational success. A group of college-bound seniors experiencing counseling evidenced less anxiety over not having made specific vocational choices by the time of high school graduation than a similar group not having counseling, but anxiety level was rejected by critics as an adequate criterion of counseling.

Obviously, all of these criteria are somewhat arbitrary. However, each is operational in that one can state how they will be measured, and practical in that each represents actual student behavior or outcomes of behavior which can be classified as defined objectives of counseling. Regardless of the theoretical constructs used to explain the diminishing of antisocial behavior in the first example, the actual change was beneficial to the boy. Amount of income, in spite of its many limitations as a measure of success, is certainly meaningful within our culture as a practical indication of one's ability to make effective decisions. Similarly, in the light of many considerations, it is unrealistic for many college students to worry over not having made specific vocational choices by the time they graduate from high school. Possibly, out of counseling research employing practical behavior criteria will come more information, not only for developing counseling procedures, but for developing more adequate theoretical bases from which other research may stem.

## METHODOLOGY

Among the major stumbling blocks encountered by school counselors in their research efforts are often problems in the area of design and methodology. The complexity of variables that enter into almost any counseling research problem make it difficult to design studies with which the worker can feel comfortable. Adding further frustration is the relatively low level of operational facility regarding statistical procedures, machine data processing technique, and the like, that is typical of most high school counselors. While these are very real problems, they are not insurmountable, and need not prevent counselors from engaging in meaningful research and development. The following comments are offered as suggestions for overcoming these difficulties.

There are two general and rather obvious means of avoiding methodological frustrations in local research. Quite simply stated, these are (1) keep it simple, and (2) obtain competent assistance. Keeping it simple suggests that one attack very specific and practical problems of counseling. Problems of design usually vary with the scope of the study. Thus, rather than attempting to determine the effects of counseling in general, it is more sensible to study the extent to which specific objectives of counseling are being achieved in a particular school. The first and perhaps most difficult task in conducting a local study is developing a clear statement of the problem to be studied. Once this has been accomplished in terms of practical operational criteria (as discussed above), the hard part is finished and one has some assurance that the actual study can be accomplished without major setbacks.

Incidentally, this suggests a common weakness in local counseling evaluations. The shotgun approach, that is, taking a broad look without having anything very specific to look for, and hoping that something will be discovered, demands a great deal more skill, perceptive ability, and experience than does a more structured approach. Also, one should not confuse research with evaluation. Evaluation involves the concepts of good and bad, adequate and inadequate. These concepts must always involve the making of personnel judgments about certain observations. It seems only reasonable to insist that evaluation should be based on objective measurement. For example, the determination that 25 percent more counseled students than students not counseled achieved up to expectation is simply a fact. There is nothing inherently good or bad about the fact itself. To say that the fact is good, is to evaluate it in terms of some arbitrary set of values.

The second aid in methodology of local research projects, competent assistance, can be obtained from textbooks, colleagues, local supervisors, state department consultants, industrial personnel, and university and college research personnel, to name the major sources. Most of these sources are obvious, and deserve little more than brief mention here. Talking a problem over with a fellow faculty member, perhaps one who has specific research skills, can be very helpful, both in clarifying one's thoughts and in obtaining needed information. The independent use of textbooks on design and statistical procedures has obvious limitations, but nevertheless offers real potential for assistance. More and more, local and state supervisory positions are being filled with people who have research preparation and interest, and thus offer increasingly valuable sources of assistance. The very responsibilities involved in such positions, however, impose limitations on the extent to which most of these people can become involved in local research.

The two remaining sources of assistance deserve added attention. Cooperation between schools and industry has existed to some extent for many years. Recently, however, industrial firms and school systems in communities throughout the country have made concentrated and varied efforts to cooperate toward achieving mutual objectives. Add to this development the expansion of social science research in industry and it is not difficult to perceive the potential research assistance available to school counselors. In California, for example, the author and several of his colleagues have found many industries anxious to make their own research personnel available to consult with school people struggling with local research problems. Besides its interest in maintaining good public relations, the management has a sincere desire to be of assistance in discovering more effective ways of helping young people develop. Counselors should not feel hesitant about seeking competent assistance from industry when it is available.

Considering the research functions of colleges and universities, the research responsibilities of many professors in the field of guidance and counseling who have limited access to high school students, and finally, the research orientation to university professors that graduate study brings to many counselors, it is difficult to understand why university personnel and school counselors have not engaged in more cooperative research than is apparent. University personnel are perhaps the single most valuable source of research assistance to school counselors. In working with them, counselors have something to offer in return for methodological assistance, namely, a research laboratory full of almost every variety of student known. There are some indications that greater cooperation is now taking place. Again in California, for example, the 1958 National Defense Education Act promoted the school consultant business to new heights. In addition to making innumerable school surveys, many college people provided valuable assistance in helping counselors initiate meaningful local research projects. Some university people have also been able to stimulate research interest among school faculties, counseling staffs, and other school groups. It is reasonable to assume that similar things are happening throughout the country. There is no need, however, to assign the initial responsibility to the university people. Rather, school counselors who are faced with counseling problems every day need to define these problems clearly and communicate with university research people regarding their study. Besides attending classes, there are several excellent means of initiating such contacts. Local and regional professional organizations, such as the American Personnel and Guidance Association and its various divisions, hold conferences attended by both university and school guidance people, which offer both formal and informal opportunities to discuss research problems.

If we are to increase our knowledge significantly about school counseling within the coming few years, high school counselors must assume greater responsibility for initiating research.

## SUGGESTED LOCAL RESEARCH PROJECTS

This final section of Chapter 8 consists of several brief descriptions of illustrative counseling research projects which counselors might carry out "on the job." The projects are not very complex and all involve activities typically engaged in by most secondary school counselors. The descriptions are not intended to be fully developed research proposals. In each example, the problem is stated, the criterion is defined, and a general procedure is suggested. A worthwhile activity for the reader might be to list alternative criteria and outline in some detail procedural and analytical possibilities for one or more examples.

*Problem:* What effect can counseling have on students who evidence high potential for dropping out of high school?

Although in certain instances, students who withdraw from school before graduation probably benefit from their action, the majority of drop-outs in most secondary schools would benefit more from persisting in school. Counseling is frequently suggested as a means of helping students persist in school. It is important that the assumption be tested.

*Criterion:* The criterion is the number of counseled students remaining in school.

*Procedure:* This study would be designed to cover at least one school year. First-year students would be surveyed to determine which ones did not intend to finish school. To a list of such students would be added the names of those whose failing grades made early withdrawal seem probable, and the names of those whose discipline records suggested early withdrawal, both voluntary and involuntary.

From this list, counselors would eliminate the names of students for whom the school had no appropriate program of instruction. Low measured intelligence alone, of course, would not be sufficient reason for excluding a student from the list, since a school might have an extensive and well-developed program for such students.

Students remaining on the list would then be put in one of three groups on a random basis. The treatment for each of the three groups might be as follows:

Group I. Each student would be given opportunities for counseling on a systematic basis. That is, even when a student declined the initial invitation, the counselor would contact him again and extend further opportunities. In addition to counseling with students in this group, counselors would make every effort to provide assistance from various referral sources as needed. All of this would be in addition to the treatment normally extended to potential drop-outs.

Group II. Students in this group would be given no special treatment other than that normally provided students evidencing high drop-out potential. If, for example, such students were normally referred to deans, given disciplinary treatment, assigned detention time, or the like, then Group II students would receive the same treatment.

Group III. This would constitute a control group and would be offered neither the typical nor the special counseling treatment.

At the end of the year, the drop-out frequencies among the three groups would be compared. In addition, various measures of adjustment and achievement might also be compared, assuming, of course, that before and after measures had been made. Analyses ranging from simple percentage comparisons to sophisticated statistical procedures could be employed, depending upon the skills of the counselors and the help available to them. The results would help to determine the effect of counseling on persistence in school, and, depending upon the extent of analysis, could suggest more definite questions for investigation. Follow-ups could be made to determine the stability of persistence.

*Problem:* What influence does counseling have on high-ability underachievers?

*Criterion:* Decrease in discrepancy between expected and obtained achievement, using standardized measures of both, e.g., Henman-Nelson Test of Mental Ability and Iowa Tests of Educational Development composite score.

*Procedure:* Starting with the assumption that the inadequate achievement of many high-ability underachievers is due to personal problems, this study would attempt to identify the problems and help the students solve them, and would then observe changes, if any, in achievement.

The school would first define underachieving and then develop a list of all so defined high-ability underachievers. For example, all students scoring at or above the 85 percentile on the Henman-Nelson, and scoring a given number of standard score points below their Henman-Nelson percentile on the ITED, might be so defined. Obviously, this would be an extremely gross measure of underachievement. More definitive expectancy scores could be developed.

Depending upon the number of students listed, and the available counseling time, either all students listed, or a random sample of them, would be selected as the final sample. The students would then be assigned at random to a counseled and a noncounseled group. The counseled group would be given systematic opportunities for counseling; the noncounseled group would not. At the end of the school year, discrepancies between expected and obtained achievement for the groups, at the beginning and end of the study, would be compared. More definitive comparisons could also be made, e.g., by sex, kinds of personal problems, level of educational aspiration, or extent of extrinsic motivation, depending upon the research resources available. In addition, students in the two groups could be followed up at regular intervals in order to determine the stability of changes and any differences not evident on a short-term basis.

*Problem:* What influence can counseling have on students whose nonacceptable classroom behavior (to teachers) could cause them to be identified as "trouble makers," "show-offs," "smart alecks," or the like?

Certainly, the terms given are stereotypes. Students so classified by teachers represent a multitude of personal and social problems. However, because they interfere with good classroom management, their nonacceptable social behavior prevents them from making full use of educational opportunities. Regardless of the causes and cores of their manifested behavior, it is generally beneficial for them to modify it. For purposes of school morale, if for no other reason, in most schools such students must be given disciplinary treatment.

*Criterion:* Teacher ratings of student social behavior in classes.

*Procedure:* At the completion of approximately six weeks of school, teachers would be asked to submit the names of students having difficulty adjusting to classroom procedures. Teachers would then be given instruction in filling out rating scales, and would then be asked to complete either an original or commercially available rating scale for the students they had named. Teachers would also be asked to write a brief description of their perceptions of each student's problem, and provide examples of how they were manifested.

The students then would be divided at random into a counseled and noncounseled group; the former would be offered systematic counseling and the latter would not. At the end of the school year, the teacher would be asked to repeat the initial appraisal procedures for both groups, and a comparison of before and after ratings and observations would be made. If more measures were taken, more extensive analyses would be possible.

*Problem:* What influence can counseling have on self-acceptance as reflected in educational plans?

One of the goals of counseling is to help students accept their various characteristics. A counseling staff can and should attempt to determine the extent to which it is achieving this goal. As pointed out in an earlier chapter, students can understand without accepting. One indication of acceptance is the degree to which information about oneself is reflected in observable behavior.

*Criterion:* Changes from inappropriate to more appropriate educational choices as judged by counselors.

*Procedure:* A group of students would be allowed to make educational plans for high school without counseling and with minimum assistance from teachers. Plans would be made from printed course descriptions, on the basis of the self-concepts each student maintained. The counseling staff would then examine the stated educational plans of each student in the light of student aptitude and achievement appraisal data, and, using some agreed-upon criteria, would list students who made seriously inappropriate choices. Two groups would then be formed on a random basis: a counseled and a noncounseled group. Students in the former group would then be offered systematic counseling, and those in the latter would not. During counseling, students would be given appraisal information and, of course, encouraged to discuss the meaning and implications of the data. Students would not be asked to revise their plans at the time counseling was terminated. Some time after termination of counseling, perhaps eight or nine weeks later, both the counseled and noncounseled students would be asked to restate their educational plans, using the same materials as before the counseling. Counselors would examine the new plans and compare the changes, if any, between the two groups. The analysis could be extended easily so as to examine differences in changes between those originally choosing too ambitious a program as opposed to those choosing a program below their potential. The results would be one indication of the extent to which counseling helped the students accept information about themselves.

*Problem:* Is educational counseling with junior high school students who are planning their high school programs more effective when done by junior high or senior high counselors?

Both methods suggested are employed and both are defended with equal enthusiasm. The question involves several variables, two important ones being the counseling competencies of the two groups of counselors involved and the particular complexities of a given school system. If it can be assumed that no important differences in counseling competencies exist between junior and senior high school counseling staffs, then the issue might profitably be investigated by a school system. *Criterion:* Changes in programs after school begins.

*Procedure:* The procedure would be relatively simple. Ninth-grade students (or eighth-graders, as the case may be) would be divided into two groups on a random basis. Using the same materials, junior high counselors would counsel with students in one group and senior high counselors would counsel with those in the other. After school started, the frequencies of requests for course changes in the two groups would be compared. Frequency of the various reasons given for changes could also be compared for the two groups (e.g., misunderstanding of course content, misunderstanding of majors, parental opinion, or pressure, desire to be in a home room with former classmates, or desire to have lunch period with a friend).

Difference in favor of the high school counselor might suggest their doing all of the counseling, thus freeing the junior high counselor for other counseling problems. It might also suggest means by which the junior high counselor could better prepare for this particular task. On the other hand, the opposite result might suggest that the difficulties senior high counselors encounter in establishing rapport with the ninth-grader are such that they are relatively ineffective in achieving this particular task.

### Suggested References

*Research Procedures*

Edwards, Allen L., *Techniques of Attitude Scale Construction,* Appleton-Century-Crofts, 1957.

Guilford, J. P., *Fundamental Statistics in Psychology and Education,* McGraw-Hill, 1956.

Super, Donald E., *et al., Vocational Development, A Framework for Research,* Career Pattern Study Monographs, Teachers College, 1957.

*Literature Reviews*

*Review of Education Research, Guidance and Counseling,* American Educational Research Association, April, 1960.

Tyler, Leona E., *The Work of the Counselor,* Appleton-Century-Crofts, 1953. Research summaries following each chapter are only one of the many features which make this a valuable volume for counselors. Chapter XIV, "The Significance of Evaluation Studies," is of particular interest.

Mowrer, O. Hobart (ed.), *Psychotherapy, Theory, and Research,* Ronald, 1953.

# INDEX